THE GODS
WHO
WALK
AMONG US

THE GODS
WHO
WALK
AMONG US

by

Thomas R. Horn

Donald C. Jones, Ph. D.

Huntington House Publishers

Huntington House Publishers
P.O. Box 53788
Lafayette, Louisiana 70505

Library of Congress Card
Catalog Number 98-75119
ISBN 1-56384-161-4

Dedication

To the memory of William Cornish (W.C.) Jones, Charles K. (C.K.) Barnes, and Orville R. (O.R.) Cross, faithful ministers of the Gospel of Jesus Christ.

Contents

Foreword

The Gods Who Walk among Us is a most enlightening and insightful book on a subject about which we need to know more. It graphically describes the gods of this world and their wide-ranging influence upon individuals and upon peoples. This book is most unusual and timely. For the most part, today's generation is unaware of, even blind to, the dangers of ideas and teachings regarding the spirit-world that have become so commonplace. Demons, worship of demons, occult activities, and the like, have been topics somewhat apart from evangelical believer's concerns. Most of us have given little thought or study to such things. We have felt almost untouched or untainted by them. How dangerously mistaken we have been.

Authors Thomas Horn and Donald Jones have researched the subject remarkably well. Not only have they done a superb job of identifying the gods of antiquity and their functions, but they have, in scholarly fashion, shown that these same gods command the attention and allegiance of multitudes of modern men and women. While Horn and Jones suggest that the names of some of the gods may have been altered to a degree, they demonstrate quite conclusively that their nefarious activities have remained constant. After reading this book, we are suddenly aware of the "ever-present darkness" and find that we can no longer afford to be blind to what we have previously ignored. It is evident that pagan worship and rituals are going on today. Of particular interest is the revelation that all of Egypt's plagues were direct affronts to her recognized and revered deities. In every instance, we see how Jehovah effectively demonstrated his vast and unequalled superiority.

Horn and Jones recognize that the gods of this world are, in every instance, and in every manifestation, representations of the evil super-natural; in fact, they are representations of Satan himself. They believe, and with good reason, that the New Age Movement is, at its core, a cleverly devised scheme whereby Satan is seeking to acquire the allegiance of all of mankind; they provide adequate illustration to support this thesis. The suggestion that possibly some things that occur during worship times in our churches today are similar to things which happened in pagan worship is, to say the least, frightening. Horn and Jones ascribe a measure of credibility to UFO sightings, and are persuaded that the evil supernatural is making alarming and ever- increasing inroads into modern culture. They believe this sets the stage for the Antichrist. This book is an eye-opener for some of us who grew up in a day when most people believed in the God of the Bible, even if they did not strive to obey Him. No doubt we were simplistic, even naive about the spirit world, especially the evil spirit world. No longer! It is time to pay attention to what Horn and Jones say, for to be well- informed is to have the possibility of being well- prepared. We are at the end of the age. The coming of our Lord is near. Let us sound the trumpet in Zion!

R. L. Brandt

Acknowledgment

I wish to acknowledge the following people without whose help and inspiration this book would not have been possible: Dr. Donald C. and Joyce Jones for their willingness to work with me on this project. Pastor Rance and Jaynie Kinser for their unconditional love and support. Judy Vorfeld for her tireless technical and research assistance. R.L. Brandt for providing a thoughtful forward. Superintendents William O. Vickery and William I. Gallaher for their steadfast leadership example over the years. My mother Virginia (Sally) for a lifetime of love and support. My sister Vida for sharing deeply personal information on the possible spiritual aspects of the UFO abduction phenomenon. My big brother Clarence (Amil) for illustrating what it means to be a pastor. And to my wife Juanita, and our children Althia, Joe, and Donna, for being the greatest family on earth.

The Origin of the Gods

Birds skipped among groves of date palms along the marshy banks of the Euphrates in the year B.C. 3500. As the sun arose above Sumer, the alluvial desert of the Middle East came alive with agricultural activity. In a valley forged between the twin rivers of the Tigris and the Euphrates, magnificent walled cities awoke to the chatter of busy streets and marketplaces. In what the Greeks would later call "Mesopotamia" (between the rivers), the world's first great trade center and civilization developed. The opulent Sumerian cities of Ur—the home of Abram—Uruk, and Lagash, had become the economic machines of the ancient Middle East, and industries from as far away as Jericho, near the Mediterranean Sea, and Catal Huyuk, in Asia Minor, competed for the trade opportunities they provided. Laborers from the biblical city of Jericho exported salt to Sumer, and miners from Catal Huyuk prepared obsidian, used in making mirrors, for shipment to the ancient metropolis. But while the prehistoric people of the East looked to the Sumerians for their supply of daily bread, the Sumerians themselves gazed heavenward to the early rising of Utu (Shamash), the all-providing sun god, as he prepared once

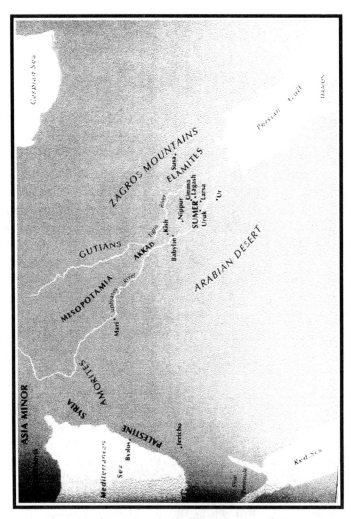

Ancient Sumeria/Mesopotamia

again to ride across the sky in his mule-drawn chariot. In B.C. 3500, Utu was not alone among the gods.

By now, the Sumerian pantheon provided the earliest known description of organized mythology, consisting of a complex system of more than 3,000 deities and covering nearly every detail of nature and human enterprise. There were gods of sunshine and rain. There were vegetation gods, fertility gods, river gods, animal gods, and gods of the afterlife. There were the great gods, Enlil (prince of the air), Anu (ruler of the heavens), Enki, (the god of water), and so on. Under these, existed a second level of deities, including Nannar, the moon god, Utu, the sun god, and Inanna, the "Queen of Heaven." But, where did the gods of Sumeria come from?

Since the religion of Sumeria was the first known organized mythology, and would greatly influence the foundational beliefs of the forthcoming nations of Assyria, Egypt, Greece, Rome, and others, this question has interested scholars and historians for more than a millennium. Specifically, where does one find the historical beginning of the ancient gods of Sumeria? Were the Sumerian deities the product of human imagination, or the distortion of some earlier prehistoric revelation? Were they the "mythologizing" of certain ancient heroes, or, as some New Age followers suggest, the result of an extra-terrestrial "alien" visitation, which gave birth to the legends and mythological gods? More importantly, did the gods of Sumeria reflect the emergence of a real and spiritual power operating through pagan dynamics, or were the gods purely the creation of primitive imagination?

These questions are both fascinating and difficult since the gods and goddesses of ancient Sumeria/Mesopotamia continue to be shrouded in a history of unknown origins. As though, out of "nowhere," the Sumerians sprang onto the scene over 5,500 years ago, bringing with them the first written language, a corpus of progressive knowledge from complicated religious concepts, and an advanced understanding of astrology, chemistry, and mathematics. The questionable origin of the Sumerian culture has caused some theorists to conclude that the gods of Sumeria, and the subsequent mythologies that grew out of them (Assyrian, Egyptian, etc.), were the diabolical scheme of a regressive and evil "supernatural presence." If this is true, does the ancient power continue to work within our world? Do primordial and living entities, once worshipped as "gods," coexist with modern man? There are three competing theories regarding the origin of the early mythological gods: 1) the Euhemerus view; 2) the New Age view; and 3) the Biblical view.

The Euhemerus view was based on the historical theories of the Greek scholar Euhemerus, who claimed that the pagan gods originated with certain ancient and famous kings who were later deified. The more widely accepted theories, the New Age view and the Biblical view, have succeeded in becoming the popular authorities regarding original paganism, and are, therefore, the focus of our attention. What can we learn from these two views?

The New Age View
Concerning the Origin of the Gods

A growing doctrine within the New Age Movement claims that the origin of the gods, and the human race, as we know it today, is the direct result of extra-terrestrial (UFO) activity. In the introduction to his bestselling book, *Chariots of the Gods?*, Erich von Daniken, who, it might be argued, is one of the fathers of the New Age Movement related to UFOs, said, "I claim that our forefathers received visits from the universe in the remote past, even though I do not yet know who these extra-terrestrial intelligences were or from which planet they came. I nevertheless proclaim that these 'strangers' annihilated part of mankind existing at the time and produced a new, perhaps the first, *homo sapiens*."[1]

As depicted in the Hollywood films *Contact* and *Close Encounters of the Third Kind,* Erich von Daniken's hypothesis took America by storm in the 1960s with the proposition that mankind was possibly the offspring of an ancient, perhaps ongoing, extra-terrestrial experiment. New Age UFO experts like Daniken assert that the gods of mythology may have been themselves evidence of, and a reaction to, an encounter with other-worldly beings. They claim that ancient men would have considered space travelers as gods and would have recorded their arrival, their experiments, and their departure, in hieroglyphs, megaliths, and stone tablets, as supernatural encounter between gods and men. Von Daniken wrote,

> While [the] spaceship disappears again into
> the mists of the universe our friends will

talk about the miracle, 'The gods were here!' . . . they will make a record of what happened: uncanny, weird, miraculous. Then their texts will relate, and drawings will show, that gods in golden clothes were there in a flying boat that landed with a tremendous din. They will write about chariots which the gods drove over land and sea, and of terrifying weapons that were like lightning, and they will recount that the gods promised to return. They will hammer and chisel in the rock pictures of what they had seen, shapeless giants with helmets and rods on their heads, carrying boxes in front of their chests; balls on which indefinable beings sit and ride through the air; staves from which rays are shot out as if from a sun .[2]

Von Daniken also claimed that the odd appearance of some of the gods, as depicted in various hieroglyphs, (human-like creatures with falcon heads; lions with heads of bulls, etc.) could be viewed as evidence that "aliens" conducted experiments of cloning and cross-mutated ancient people and animals.

Some people accept this part of Von Daniken's hypothesis as a humanistic alternative to the Biblical account of creation. It's uncertain how many people believe such a theory, but a full eighty percent of Americans claim they believe in the possibility of extra-terrestrial life. Some, like the 39 members of the Heaven's Gate cult who committed suicide in Rancho Santa Fe, California because they believed they were being summoned by a UFO trailing the Hale-Bopp Comet, subscribe

Intergalactic New Age Scientist?

to an eerie amalgam of mysticism and conventional religion. Not surprisingly, the growing interest in UFOs and the paranormal has given birth to a host of popular television specials and weekly programs depicting such other-worldly creatures and those who claim to have encountered them. One of the more disturbing aspects of such UFO phenomena are the reports, which continue to come in from around the world, of nighttime abductions by small, wide-eyed creatures who supposedly pilot UFOs, and conduct various medical experiments on their victims. The New Age Movement argues that such activity would be proof of an ongoing experiment between humans and aliens, and they note that the radical aspects of such experiments have included impregnating victims and later removing the hybrid embryos.

Ancient Chinese folklore includes stories of a distant land of "flying carts." A Sanskrit text, *The Drona Parva,* documented "dogfights" by gods in flying machines.[3] But men like Von Daniken claim that the Bible is their best advocate and is the "greatest UFO book of all time!" The "wheel" in Ezekiel 1:15; the "pillar of cloud" in Exodus 13:21-22; and Elijah's "chariot of fire" (2 Kings 2:11), are all viewed as examples of UFO sightings by New Agers. It's true that we do find a biblical record of mysterious celestial creatures invading the earth and conducting procreative experiments. In Genesis 6:4 we read, "When mankind had spread all over the world, and girls were being born, some of the supernatural beings saw that these girls were beautiful, so they took the ones they liked. In those days, and even later, there were giants [*nepheli*] on the earth who were descendants of human women and the supernatural beings" (*TEV*). But is Genesis 6 a description of reproductive experiments conducted by advanced extra-terrestrial creatures? Or is it a record of something even more sinister?

A Christian Analysis vs. the New Age View

Regardless of one's interpretation of these and other ancient records, one fact remains. Thousands of years ago, heavenly beings visited the earth. They engaged in sexual experiments resulting in a race of mutant beings called *nepheli*. The final result appears to have been an immediate judgment from God, who ordered Israel to destroy the *nepheli* and its descendants. Thousands of years later, Jesus spoke of the events that occurred during the days of Noah as being comparable to the days leading up to the rapture of the Church (Matthew 24). This prophecy is remarkable when one realizes that after God judged the celestial beings who cohabited with the Noahtic women, all such comparable activity apparently ceased until about 1940. Then, following the infamous Roswell incident which occurred in New Mexico in 1947, people from around the world began encountering strange creatures conducting procreative experiments with increasing regularity. One is forced to wonder, what's going on? Who are these creatures? Are the current UFO visitors the same as those of Noah's day? If so, what is this reproductive experimentation about? Perhaps the answer to this question (the Christian's analysis vs the New Age view on "aliens") is hidden in the first six chapters of Genesis.

Very soon after the fall of man, we find in
Genesis 3:15 the protoevangelium (the promise
that the seed of the woman would someday bring
forth a child [Jesus] capable of destroying the
serpent's [Satan's] power). In response to the
promise, supernatural beings (fallen angels?)
appeared from the heavens and performed
reproductive experiments on human women
(Genesis 6). Was Satan attempting to intercept,
pollute, and thereby destroy the righteous seed?
Was he trying to cut off the birth line of the
Messiah? Perhaps. Satan's ancient goal included
cutting off the line leading to the Messiah. Satan
led Pharaoh to destroy the Hebrew children so
the deliverer might not be born. Herod sought
the baby Jesus in the *New Testament* in order to
have Him killed. In Revelation 12, we see the
devil (dragon) waiting to destroy the messianic
seed as soon as it is born of the woman. But Dr.
I.D.E. Thomas, in his book, *The Omega Conspiracy*,
suggests that Satan had even bigger plans at work
in Genesis 6. He claims that Satan (as opposed to
aliens) was trying to produce a race of mutant
warriors by breeding fallen angels with women in
an effort to exterminate the children of God.

From a Christian's point of view, this could
explain how people like the Sumerians of
Mesopotamia, who were enemies of Yahweh, appeared out of nowhere around B.C. 3500, bringing
with them a pantheon of deities, the first written
language, and a superior knowledge of earthly
sciences. This may also explain why many of the
religions that followed Sumerian mythology, including Greek mythology, emerged from the origi-

nal idea that powerful beings, with names like "Zeus" and "Apollo," visited the earth, intermarried with women, and fathered half-human children. Dr. Thomas believes recent UFO abduction activity may point to the birth of a new race of anti-God warriors, as we approach the end of the age and the coming of Armageddon.

Does Genesis 6 support the New Age theory that alien creatures traveled from distant planets in UFOs, performed reproductive experiments on women, and were afterward honored in the images and folklore of the gods of mythology? Or, is Dr. I.D.E. Thomas correct in stating that the story in Genesis is a record of fallen angels acting in accord with Satan? What, if anything, could this tell us about the origin of the gods and the current interstellar phenomena? Are we experiencing an ongoing invasion of earth by intergalactic scientists, or is Satan busy advancing the most sophisticated con game in history? We know that the rapture of the Church will be accompanied by "fearful sights and great signs from heaven" (Luke 21:11). Perhaps Satan is contriving an "alien invasion" to explain the disappearance of so many people at once! If 80 percent of the population believes in the possibility of extra-terrestrial intelligence, wouldn't this be a powerful form of deception? Since New Age theology produces a growing belief among some contemporary church groups that flying saucers will be the method God uses to retrieve the Christian community during the Rapture, couldn't the UFO sightings phenomenon play a part in the great deception that will pervade the earth following the Rapture?

We read in 2 Thessalonians 2:8-12,

> And then shall that Wicked [one] be re-
> vealed . . . whose coming is after the work-
> ing of Satan with all power and signs and
> lying wonders. . . . And for this cause God
> shall send them strong delusion, that they
> should believe a lie: That they all might be
> damned who believed not the truth, but
> had pleasure in unrighteousness.

The world authorities remaining to make up the governments of the Antichrist will need an explanation for those taken in the Rapture. People from around the world will be missing! Now imagine if the Rapture was followed by hundreds of "space craft" landing on earth piloted by creatures who appeared to be advanced humanoids, couldn't these beings claim to have removed the Christians into some kind of a high-tech "rapture," and simultaneously present their leader (antichrist?) as the messiah? Couldn't they point to ancient mysteries, megaliths, pyramids, and the gods of mythology, as proof of an ancient visitation of planet earth?

The late Pulitzer Prize-winning author and agnostic Carl Sagan was, until his death, working on a screenplay about the ramifications of just such a savior who appears in the coming millennium![4] Humanists like Sagan argue that evidence such as the meteorite,[5] which has been hypothesized as indicating that microscopic life existed on Mars millions of years ago, is proof that prehistoric life forms could have moved throughout the universe for untold millennia. Not long ago, people who supported UFO activity were the object of scorn. Because of accumulating evidence and reputable eye-witness accounts, this is no longer the case. That some kind of unexplained phenomenon, called the UFO experience by some, occurs, is beyond question. UFO reports are coming in at the alarming world-wide rate of about six sightings per hour! Whatever or whomever they are, the reality of this activity can no longer be doubted. One concludes that these beings are either advanced humanoids from outer space, or that this activity signals an ongoing deception of demonic design. If the current UFO activity is demonic and indicates that Satan has for centuries planned an "alien" visitation in order to, among other things, explain the Rapture of the church, wouldn't it be reasonable to believe that his plans have heretofore included indoctrination and advanced intelligence? Military invasions always involve preliminary and clandestine maneuvers, and one should believe Satan's plans to deceive in the past, the present, and the future World Order, would first involve covert strategies of brainwashing, political manipulation, and the positioning of his agents in places of power.

While I believe that the New Age Movement's interpretation of UFO phenomenon and the origin of the gods is erroneous, I do credit New Agers for recognizing the high possibility that the gods of mythology were a result of, and perhaps a first step toward, the developing of the schemes of a super-intelligent force, a power which may energize the UFO phenomenon today. But what New Agers describe as the goals of a "highly advanced alien civilization," I call the plotting of an evil supernatural creature.

The Biblical View of the
Origin of the Gods

The biblical (and I believe correct) view of the origin of the pagan gods begins with Original Revelation. This means there was a perfect revelation from God to man at the time of creation. The first man, Adam, was one with God and perceived divine knowledge from the mind of God. Adam was "in tune" with the mental processes of God, and understood, therefore, what God knew about science, astronomy, cosmogony, geology, eschatology, and so on. After the fall, Adam was "detached" from the mind of God, but retained an imperfect memory of divine revelation, including a knowledge of God's plan of redemption. Two things began to occur in the decades after the Fall: 1) information from the original revelation became distant and distorted, as it was dispersed among the nations, and passed from generation to generation; and 2) the realm of Satan seized upon this opportunity to receive worship, and to turn people away from Yahweh, by distorting and counterfeiting the original revelation with pagan ideas and gods. This point of view seems reasonable when one considers that the earliest historical and archeological records, from civilizations around the world, have consistently pointed back to and repeated portions of the original story.

In their startling book, *The Discovery of Genesis*, the Rev. C.H. Kang and Dr. Ethel R. Nelson confirm that prehistoric Chinese ideographic pictures (used in very ancient Chinese writing) depict the story of Genesis, including the creation of the Man and Woman, the Garden, the Temptation and Fall, Noah's flood, and the Tower of Babel. In his book, *The Real Meaning of the Zodiac,* Dr. James Kennedy claims that the ancient signs of the Zodiac also indicate a singular and original revelation, a kind of gospel in the stars. And that the message of the stars, although demonized and converted into astrology after the Fall, originally recorded the Gospel of God. Kennedy writes:

> There exists in the writings of virtually all civilized nations a description of the major stars in the heavens, something which might be called the "Constellations of the Zodiac" or the "Signs of the Zodiac," of which there are twelve. If you go back in time to Rome, or beyond that to Greece, or before that to Egypt, Persia, Assyria, or Babylonia, regardless of how far back you go, there is a remarkable phenomenon; nearly all nations had the same twelve signs, representing the same twelve things, placed in the same order.

The book of Job, thought by many to be the oldest book of the Bible, goes back to approximately 2150 B.C., 650 years before Moses came on the scene to write the Pentateuch; over 1,100 years before Homer wrote the *Odyssey* and the *Illiad;* and 1,500 years before Thales, the first philosopher, was born. In Job 38, God finally speaks to Job and his false comforters. As He is questioning Job, showing him and his companions their ignorance, God says to them, "Canst thou bind the sweet influences of Pleiades, or loose the bands of Orion? Canst thou bring forth Mazzaroth in his season? Or canst thou guide Arcturus with his sons?"

(Job 38:31,32). We see here reference to
the constellations of Orion and Pleiades,
and the star Arcturus. Also in the book of
Job, there is reference to Cetus, the Sea
Monster, and to Draco, the Great Dragon.
I would call your attention to Job 38:32a:
"Canst thou bring forth Mazzaroth in his
season?" Mazzaroth is a Hebrew word which
means, "The Constellations of the Zodiac."
In what may be the oldest book in all of
human history, we find that the constellations of the zodiac were already clearly
known and understood.

Having made it clear that the Bible ex-
pressly, explicitly, and repeatedly condemns
what is now known as astrology, the fact
remains that there was a God-given Gospel
[universally acknowledged original revela-
tion] in the stars which lies beyond and
behind that which has now been corrupted.[6]

In his book, Kennedy strongly condemns the
practice of astrology, while asserting his view that
the constellations of the zodiac were likely given
by God to the first man as "record-keepers" of the
original revelation of God. If the primary assump-
tion of the Biblical view is correct, that an original
revelation was corrupted after the fall of man and
subsequently degenerated into the mythologies of
the pagan gods, one should be able to find numerous examples of such corruption from the
beginning of history, in various civilizations around
the world.

   Since the myths behind the gods would thus
be "borrowed" ideas, the corrupted texts would be
similar to the original truth, and, in that sense,

evidence of a singular and original revelation. Furthermore, if the distortions of the original revelation were in fact energized by an evil supernaturalism, the goal of the alterations would be to draw people away from the worship of Yahweh. In certain ancient legends, such as the *Enuma Elish,* the *Adapa Epic,* and the *Epic of Gilgamesh,* we discover early traces of the kaleidoscope of the original revelation, plagiarized for the purpose of constructing the mythologies of the pagan gods.

Early Traces of Corruption

Evidence suggests that the earliest legends of mythology were preceded by a belief in "the God" (*Yahweh* to the Hebrews) as the creator of all things and the "ruler of heaven." Later, Satan was described as "the god of this world" (2 Cor. 4:4), and the "prince of the air" (Eph. 2:2). A fascinating struggle between the "ruler of the heavens" versus the "power of the air" occurred in early Sumerian mythology after Enki, the god of wisdom and water, created the human race out of clay. It appears that Anu, who was at first the most powerful of the Sumerian gods and the "ruler of the heavens," was superseded in power and popularity by Enlil, the "god of the air." To the Christian mind this is perceived as nothing less than Satan, the god of the air, continuing his pretence to the throne of God, and his usurpation of Yahweh, "the Lord of the heavens." It also indicates a corruption of the original revelation and perhaps an effort on the part of Satan to trick the pagan Sumerians into perceiving him as the "supreme" god (above the God of Heaven) and, therefore, worthy of adoration.

Correspondingly, in the *Enuma Elish* (a Babylonian epic), Marduk, the great god of the city of Babylon, was exalted above the benevolent gods and extolled as the creator of the world. Marduk was symbolized as a dragon (as is Satan in Revelation 12:9) called the *Muscrussu,* and his legend appears to contain several distortions of the important elements of the biblical account of creation. The *Adapa Epic* tells of another Babylonian legend that is also roughly equivalent to the Genesis account of creation. In it, Adapa, like Adam, underwent a test on food consumption, failed the test, and forfeited his opportunity for immortality. As a result of the failure, suffering and death were passed along to humanity.

Finally, the *Epic of Gilgamesh* is a Sumerian poem, which, like the *Adapa Epic,* is deeply rooted in ancient Assyrian and Babylonian mythology. In 1872, George Smith discovered the Gilgamesh tablets while doing research on the Assyrian library of Ashurbanipal at the British Museum. Because of the strong similarity to the biblical account of Noah and the great flood, Bible scholars have viewed the Gilgamesh epic with interest (and suspicion) since its discovery. As the legend goes, Gilgamesh, the king of the city of Uruk, was told about the flood from his immortal friend, Utnapishtim (the Sumerian equivalent of Noah). Utnapishtim described for Gilgamesh how the great god Enlil decided to destroy all of mankind because of its "noisy" sins. A plague was sent but failed to persuade mankind of better behavior, and, consequently, the gods decided on a complete extermination of the human race. Enki, the lord of the waters, was not happy with the other gods for this decision and warned Utnapishtim of the coming deluge, instructing him to tear down his house and build a great boat. Utnapishtim obeyed Enki, built a great vessel, and sealed it with pitch and bitumen. The family of Utnapishtim loaded onto the boat together with various beasts and fowl. When the rains came, the doors were closed and the vessel rose up above the waters. Like Noah, Utnapishtim sent out a dove, and later a swallow, to search for dry land. They both returned. Later, a raven was released and it never came back. After several more days the boat came to rest on the top of a mountain where Utnapishtim built an altar and offered a sacrifice of thanksgiving to the gods. As the gods smelt the sweet offering, all but Enlil repented for sending the flood.

In my first book, *Spiritual Warfare, The Invisible Invasion,* I described an interesting example of the original revelation of God as distorted and plagiarized by Satan in order to draw men away from the worship of Jehovah. Concerning Asclepius, the Greek god of healing, I wrote:[7]

> At the base of Pergamums hill stood the shrine of Asclepius, equipped with its own library, theater, sleeping chambers used in healing rituals, and long underground tunnels joining various other shrines to which pagans journeyed to receive the healing powers of Apollo's favorite son. The Christian Church considered these mystical powers as demonic, for the worship of Asclepius focused on the image of a serpent, sometimes called Glycon, an enormous serpent-figure some historians see as the origin for the modern symbol of healing, a serpent

winding about a pole. Asclepius carried the
lofty title, the hero god of healing. In Numbers 21, Moses designed the brazen serpent on a pole that was used of God as an
oracle of healing. Seven hundred and forty-
three years later, in 2 Kings 18:4, we find
that Israel had began to worship the brazen serpent with offerings and incense.

From here the image was adopted into
Greek mythology where it became the symbol of Asclepius, the Greek god of healing.
Asclepius was reported to have cured untold numbers from every conceivable disease, even raising a man from the dead.
This caused Apollo, through his Oracle at
Delphi, to declare, "Oh Asclepius! Thou
who art born a great joy to all mortals,
whom lovely Coronis bare to me, the child
of love, at rocky Epidaurus." Such a healer
was he reported to be, that Pluto, god of
Hades, complained to Zeus that hardly
anyone was dying anymore, and so Zeus
destroyed Asclepius with a thunderbolt. Afterward, Apollo pleaded with Zeus to restore his son and this intercession so moved
Zeus that he not only brought Asclepius
back to life, but immortalized him as the
god of medicine.

First at Thessaly, and finally throughout
the Greek and Roman world, Asclepius was
worshiped as the god of healing.

Thus, we find a glaring example of God's "revelation" plagiarized for demonic purposes. Greek
mythology represented Asclepius had the power
to heal the sick and bring the dead back to life by

drawing blood from the side´ of the goddess of justice. Asclepius was symbolized by a serpent winding about a pole, and he was called the great "Physician." The obvious intention of the serpent on a pole in Numbers 21 was to focus mankind on the coming Messiah, the true Great Physician, who would hang upon a pole and would deliver His followers from sickness and death by the blood that ran from His side.

The Energy of the Gods

Time does not allow for a full disclosure of the many other examples of corruption that occurred with regard to the Original Revelation. They include distortions or "knock-offs" of the virgin birth, Heaven and Hell, the Resurrection and Final Judgment, water baptism, communion, etc. In addition to the corruptions of the original revelation which pre-dated the gods of mythology, the Biblical view of the origin of the gods makes the following important assumptions: 1) that there exists within our universe real and supernatural powers; 2) that these powers are divided by their nature into two separate camps or "kingdoms," one evil, the other good; 3) that these kingdoms are presided over by rulers, the biblical Satan over the evil and Yahweh over the good; and 4) that the kingdom of Satan provided the historical energy or "life" within and behind the gods of mythology as Satan's kingdom solicited human worship through the elements of idolatry.

Quoting again from *Spiritual Warfare, The Invisible Invasion,* I conclude:

> The worship of Asclepius and other such idolatries were, as Paul would later articu-

late in 1 Corinthians 10:20, *the worship of demons.* [emphasis added] In Acts 7:41-42, we find that when men serve idols they are worshiping "the army of heaven" (Jerusalem Bible). Psalms 96:5 says, "For all the gods of the nations are idols" (*'elilim, LXX daimonia*). Demons. Many other biblical references indicate evil supernaturalism as the true dynamic of idolatry and reveal that idols of stone, flesh, or other imagery are simply "elilim (empty, nothing, vanity), but that *behind these images exist the true objects of heathen adoration: demons.*"

John Milton wrote in *Paradise Lost* that millions of spiritual creatures walk the earth unseen. The Biblical view of the origin of the gods affirms the idea that "in the beginning" Yahweh created the heavens (celestial beings, planets, etc.) and the earth. Lucifer, "the light bearer," was a crowning achievement of God's heavenly creation and a chief servant of the creative Yahweh. But Lucifer became jealous of the worship Yahweh was receiving from his many creations, and proudly proclaimed, "I will exalt my throne above the stars of God. . . . I will be like the most high" (Isa.14:13-14). Somehow Lucifer convinced one-third of the celestial creatures to join him in a great rebellion, with the uprising ultimately resulting in Lucifer and his followers being cast out of Heaven. Lucifer (now Satan), driven by a quest for worship and thirsty for revenge against Yahweh, tempted Eve, and, after the fall with its resulting separation between man and God, moved to corrupt the divine truths contained within the Original Revelation by proclaiming himself (the god of the air) more worthy of worship than the God of Heaven.

If such a summary of the Biblical view is correct, that a real and evil supernatural presence exists and has for centuries drawn men away from worshipping Yahweh through the dynamics of various mythologies, the following questions arise: Were the angels that joined Lucifer in the fall also driven by a lust for worship? Did the images and attributes ascribed to the gods of mythology reflect the real and spiritual characteristics of certain unseen personalities operating behind them? More important, is the kingdom of Satan still at work in this manner? Do the living entities of the ancient gods continue to walk among us? If so, do such spirits embody themselves in trees, earth, and idols of stone, or should we assume that modern idolatry has acquired a more selective sophistication and social manifestation? In the following chapters, we'll search for the answers to these questions through a comparison of the various aspects of the gods of mythology. But, be warned, the forthcoming conclusions may startle you.

Notes

1. Erich von Daniken, *Chariots of the Gods* (G.P. Putnam's Sons, New York, 1970), 10.

2. Ibid., 26

3. Jason McManus, *The UFO Phenomenon: Mysteries of the Unknown* (Time Life Books, Alexandria, VA, 1987), 12.

4. The Hollywood Reporter, *The Oregonian* (9 August 1996), Arts & Entertainment Guide, 26.

5. John Noble Wilford, *The Oregonian* (7 August

1996), Front Page.

6. Dr. James Kennedy, Ph. D., *The Real Meaning of the Zodiac* (TCRM Publishing, Ft. Lauderdale, FL, 1993), 6-8.

7. Thomas R. Horn, *Spiritual Warfare—The Invisible Invasion* (Lafayette, LA: Huntington House Publishers, 1998), 21-22.

8. Ibid., 24.

The Gods Who Walked among the Egyptians

"Oh Egypt! Egypt! Your knowledge will survive but in legends, which later generations will be unable to believe."

—Lucius Apuleius,
Roman Philosopher,
Second Century A.D.

As the centuries passed by, the god and goddess worshipping cities of the Sumerians began to fade away. The flourishing fields of agriculture that provided the underpinnings of the great Sumerian economy were depleted of fertility through over-irrigation, and residues of salt build-up appeared to chafe the surface of the land. The city-states of Sumeria, Kish, Ur, Lagash, and Umma, weakened by a millennium of ruthless infighting among the Sumerians, finally succumbed to militant external forces. The barbarian armies of the Elamites (Persians) invaded and destroyed the city of Ur, and Amorites from the west overran the northern province of Sumer and subsequently established the hitherto little-known town of Babylon as their capital.

By B.C.1840, Hammurabi, the sixth king of
Babylon, conquered the remaining cities of
Sumeria and forged northern Mesopotamia and
Sumeria into a single nation. But the ultimate
demise of the Sumerian people did not vanquish
their ideas. Sumerian art, language, literature, and,
especially, religion, had been forever absorbed into
the cultures and social academics of the nations
surrounding Mesopotamia, including the Hittite
nation, the Babylonians, and the ancient Assyrians.
A principal benefactor of Sumeria's ideas, and a
people who would ultimately make their own
contributions to the ancient mythologies, was an
old and flourishing population of agrarians known
as the Egyptians.

By the year B.C. 1350, Egyptian dominance
had spread from Syria and Palestine into the far-
thest corners of the Fertile Crescent. From northern Mesopotamia to the Baltic Sea, the pharaohs
of Egypt had established themselves as the social
and economic leaders of the civilized world, rul-
ing an area more than 2,000 miles in length. The
military superiority of the Egyptian army demonstrated its ability to subdue the threat of resistance, maintaining a hegemony that extended from
the Nubians to the Hyksos. But, in the final analysis, it was the influence of the gods of Egypt, with
their magic, myths, and rituals, that provided the
Egyptians with a lasting place in history and led
the following generations into an immense, enlightening description of the ancient mythologies,
including a wealth of information regarding the
dynamics and supernatural possibilities of paganism.

Thoth, by Brooke Townsend

Facts about Atum (RA), Osiris, and Isis

Prehistoric Egyptians believed in the same fundamental idea that most evolutionists subscribe to today, the premise that the oceans both preceded, and, in some way, contributed to the creation of the living cosmos. From the Fifth Dynasty Pyramid Texts, the Heliopolitan theory of creation stated that Atum (the sun god, Ra) independently created himself from a singular expression of self will, an act visualized by the Egyptians as a divine egg that appeared upon the primordial waters of the all-filling ocean called Nun, out of which Atum (meaning "He who created himself"), emerged. According to myth, a second act of creation developed around a divine masturbation when Atum, the great "He-She," orally copulated himself and afterward regurgitated his children, Shu and Tefnut, who assumed the positions of god and goddess of air and moisture.

Later, when Shu and Tefnut became lost in the universal ocean of Nun, Atum exhibited his paternal care by sending out his Eye, which had the curious habit of detaching itself from Atum and thinking independent thoughts, to look for them. The Eye of Atum succeeded in finding the child gods and eventually returned to discover that Atum had grown impatient during the wait and had created a second eye. In order to placate the hostility that soon developed between the two divine eyes, Atum affixed the first eye upon his forehead where it was to oversee and rule the forthcoming world of creation. Thus, the Eye of Atum became the jealous, destructive aspect of the sun god Ra.

To avoid getting lost again in the all-filling waters of Nun, Shu and Tefnut procreated Geb (the earth), and Nut (the sky), and thus provided the more stable elements of earth, nature, and the seasons. Later, Geb was conceptualized as cohabiting with Nut and producing four children of his own: Seth, Osiris, Isis, and Nephthys. Of these, Osiris and Isis grew into such important cult deities that the mythology of the Egyptian religion was modified to support the claim that Osiris, with the help of his sister-wife Isis, had nearly overthrown and replaced Ra as the most powerful of the gods, an action that so enraged his brother Seth that the hateful and jealous sibling killed him.

Seth's murderous act was followed by the jackal-headed god, Anubis, assisting Isis with the embalming of her slain husband-brother Osiris, an act which secured the jackal god's position as "the god of embalming." Then, while still in mourning, Isis summoned the wisdom of Thoth, which she combined with her own proficient magical skills and produced a resurrected Osiris, who, in turn, impregnated her with Horus, the god of daylight. Horus promptly avenged his father's death by killing the evil brother Seth. Another version of the myth claims that Horus was born to Isis only after she impregnated herself with semen, which she took from the corpse of Osiris. Yet another story claims that Seth persuaded his brother Osiris to climb into a box, which he quickly shut and threw into the Nile. Osiris drowned and his body floated down the Nile river where it snagged on the limbs of a tamarisk tree. In Byblos, Isis recovered the body from the river bank and

took it into her care. In her absence, Seth stole the
body again and chopped it into fourteen pieces,
which he threw into the Nile. Isis searched the
river bank until she recovered every piece, except
for the genitals, which had been swallowed by a
fish (Plutarch says a crocodile). But Isis simply
replaced the missing organ with a facsimile and
was somehow able to reconstruct Osiris and im-
pregnate herself with the ithyphallic corpse.

This portion of the Isis/Osiris myth probably
developed over time in order to provide the legendary background necessary to sanction the kind
of temple prostitution practiced during the rituals
of Isis. Temple prostitutes represented the human
manifestation of the goddess and were available
for ritual sex as a form of imitative magic. Much
of the details are no longer available, but it appears these prostitutes usually began their services
to the goddess as a child and were deflowered at
a very young age by a priest, or, as Isis was, by a
carved phallus of the god Osiris. Sometimes prostitutes were chosen, on the basis of their beauty,
as the sexual mates of the sacred temple bulls.
Such bulls were considered the incarnation of
Osiris. In other places, such as at Mendes, temple
prostitutes were offered in coitus to divine goats.[1]

Regardless, from this time forward Osiris was
considered the chief god of the deceased and the
judge of the netherworld, the dark and dreary
underworld region of the dead. In human form
Osiris was perceived as a mummy and, paradoxi-
cally, while he was loved as the guarantor of life
after death, he was feared as the demonic presence that decayed the bodies of the dead. Such
necromantic worship of Osiris and Isis grew to

become an important part of several Mediterranean religions, with the most famous cult center of Osiris at Abydos in Upper Egypt, where an annual festival reenacted his death and resurrection. In Abydos, Osiris was called the god of the setting sun, the mysterious "force" that ruled the region of the dead just beneath the western horizon. He was venerated in this way primarily because death, and specifically the fear of one's estate after death, grew to consume so much of Egyptian consciousness.

In the funerary texts, known as the *Book of the Dead,* the most elaborate magical steps were developed around the Osiris myth to assist the Egyptians with their journey into the afterlife. It was believed that every person had a *Ka,* a spiritual and invisible duplicate, and that such *Ka* accompanied them throughout eternity. Since the *Ka* provided each person with a resurrected body in the kingdom of the dead, but could not exist without the maintenance of the earthly body, every effort was made to preserve the human corpse. The body was, therefore, mummified according to the elaborate magic rituals passed down from Isis, who, according to legend, singularly perfected the rituals of mummification through her work on Osiris. Wooden replicas of the body were also placed in the tomb, as a kind of substitute in case the mummy was accidently destroyed, and additional protection for the corpse was provided through the construction of ingenious burial tombs specifically designed to hide and preserve the human body for eternity. Finally, curses were placed throughout the tomb, as a warning against intruders.

At death of the Egyptian, *Ka* departed from the human body and, accompanied by the hymns and prayers of the living, used the formulas memorized from the funerary texts to outsmart the horrible demons seeking to impede the *Ka's* progress into the kingdom (or hall) of Osiris. Arriving at the judgment hall, the heart of the *Ka* was "weighed in the balance" by Osiris and his forty-two demons. If they found the deceased lacking in virtue, he was condemned to an eternity of hunger and thirst. If the *Ka* was determined to have belonged to an outright "sinner," it was cut to pieces and fed to Ammit, the miserable little goddess and "eater of souls." But if the deceased was judged to have lived a virtuous life, the *Ka* was granted admission into the heavenly fields of Yaru, where foods were abundant and pleasures unending. The only toil in this heaven was to serve in the grain fields of Osiris, and even this could be obviated by placing substitutionary statues, called *shawabty*, into the tomb.

There is some evidence that the forty-two demons or "judges" of Osiris were in some way related to the prehistoric legend of the Watchers, the mysterious angelic beings who first appeared in the early cultures of the Middle East. The Egyptian people originally migrated from the biblical land of Shin'ar, which means the "Land of the Watchers." The Egyptians called it *Ta Neter*, the Land of the Watchers "from which the gods came into Egypt." As mentioned in Chapter One, it's possible that a historical event occurred giving birth to the legend of the Watchers, and references to a race of "watcher/gods" who cohabited with women and sought to control the human race is attested to by numerous ancient texts. The Sumerian scribes referred to the watchers as *Anunnaki,* who, they said, "came from Nibiru" to judge/rule the inhabitants of the earth. Some have interpreted Nibiru as "a distant planet," but the actual translation is, "Those Who from Heaven to Earth Came." In the Bible, references are made to the Anakim and to the Nephilm, which also means "those who came from Heaven to Earth." In the *Book of the Dead,* there are prayers for deliverance from the Watchers (Tchatcha, the princes of Osiris), who came from Ta-Ur, the "Far Away Land," and in the Book of Jubilees, also known as the Apocalypse of Moses, the Watchers are compared to the "supernatural beings" mentioned in Genesis 6 as having come down from heaven to cohabit with women, a union ultimately leading to the birth of the giants. The Apocryphal Book of Enoch also associates the creatures of Genesis 6 with the Watchers.

We read:

> And I, Enoch, was blessing the Lord of majesty and the King of the ages, and lo! the Watchers called me, Enoch the scribe, and said to me: Enoch, thou scribe of righteousness, go, declare to the Watchers of the heaven who have left the high heaven, the holy eternal place, and have defiled themselves with women, and have done as the children of earth do, and have taken unto themselves wives: Ye have wrought great destruction on the earth: And ye shall have no peace nor forgiveness of sin: and inasmuch as they delight themselves in their children, The murder of their beloved ones

Isis, by Brooke Townsend

shall they see, and over the destruction of their children shall they lament, and shall make supplication unto eternity, but mercy and peace shall ye not attain. (1 Enoch 10:3-8)

From the *Dead Sea Scrolls,* we learn that only 200 of the larger group of powerful angels called "Watchers" ever departed from the higher Heavens and sinned. Thus, Enoch referred to the Watchers in the High Heavens as separate from the ones on earth. The fallen class of Watchers are considered by some to be the creatures referred to in the Book of Jude as the "angels which kept not their first estate, but left their own habitation . . . [and are] reserved in everlasting chains under darkness unto the judgment of the great day" (Jude 6). In either case, it appears the early Egyptian scribes believed that leaders from among the fallen Watchers had become the underworld demons of Osiris whose "terrible knives" exacted judgment upon the *Ka* of the wicked. The Egyptians were desperately afraid of these netherworld "watchers," and a significant amount of time was spent determining how to placate the judgment of Osiris and his forty-two demons. The worship of Isis, the sister-wife of Osiris, thus became integral.

As one of the most important goddesses of ancient mythology, Isis was venerated by the Egyptians, Greeks, and the Romans, as the "goddess of a thousand names," and as the undisputed queen of magical skills. Her enchantments were so powerful that she even forced the reluctant sun god Ra to reveal his most secret name. She accomplished this by conjuring a magic serpent that bit the sun god, a reptile whose venom was so potent that it brought Ra to the point of death, thus he surrendered his hidden and powerful name to the goddess. In response, Isis uttered secret words which drove the serpent's poison from Ra's body. Afterward, the victorious goddess celebrated by adding Ra's powerful and hidden name to her archive of divine words.

Such magic words (of Isis) were considered by the Egyptians to be of the highest importance for the preparation and navigation of this world and the afterlife. This was because Isis not only possessed secret words, but she instructed her followers how, when, and with what vocal tones they were to be uttered. If the proper words were pronounced perfectly—at the right time of day and with the proper ceremony, they would have the effect of altering reality, manipulating the laws of physics, and forcing the being or object to which they were directed into compliance, including evil spirits.

An example of this form of magic is found in the *Theban Recension* of the *Book of the Dead* and depicts Isis providing a spell for controlling the forty-two demons of Osiris. The formula consisted of an amulet made of carnelian that had been soaked in the water of ankhami flowers. It was supposed to be placed around the neck of the dead person, in combination with the spoken words of magic. If performed properly, it would empower the *Ka* of the individual to enter into the region of the dead under the protection of Isis, where the *Ka* would thereafter move about whenever it wanted without fear of the forty-two demons of Osiris. The only Egyptian who did not benefit from this spell was the Pharaoh, and for a very good reason. Although Pharaoh was considered to be the "son of the sun god" (Ra) and the incarnation of the falcon god Horus during his lifetime, he was considered, at death, to have become the Osiris, the divine judge of the netherworld. On earth, Pharaoh's son and predecessor would take his place as the newly anointed manifestation of Horus, and, thus, each new generation of the pharaohs provided the gods with a divine spokesman for the present world and the afterlife.

Judgment of the Egyptian God King

While conducting a recent tour of Egypt and the Holy Land, Donald C. Jones (Ph.D. in Biblical History and contributing author of this book), stood outside the Great Pyramid in Giza and pondered what it must have been like to be an Egyptian Pharaoh. As the divine son of Ra, Pharaoh was the earthly representative of the supreme god of cosmic deities; in short, Pharaoh was god on earth. Dr. Jones wondered what the children of Israel must have thought when Moses challenged the mighty arm of a ruler whose kingdom was so vast and powerful. Who would "take on" the leader of a people capable of building a single structure over thirty times larger than the Empire State Building? The Great Pyramid was built over 4,500 years ago of more than 2,000,000 blocks of stone weighing between 2 and 60 tons each, by builders whose knowledge of the earth and the planetary systems was so advanced that the Great Pyramid faces true North, South, East, and West, while also standing at the exact center of the Earth's land mass and at a height exactly that of the earth's

Dr. Jones in Egypt

mean sea level. One would understand how the leader of such a people would have easily been considered by the ancients as a god on earth.

Whereas most scholars believe that the Great Pyramid, the last standing monument of the Seven Wonders of the Ancient World, was built around the year B.C. 2560, by Khufu (Cheops), the Pharaoh of the Fourth Egyptian Dynasty, and that Moses probably challenged the pharaoh, known as Ramses II, many other testaments, temples, and pyramids, have survived to reveal that each of the Pharaohs were, in their respective times (at least in the mind of the average Egyptian), the undisputed god-kings of planet earth. Nevertheless, God instructed Moses to go "unto Pharaoh . . . [and] bring forth my people the children of Israel out of Egypt" (Exod. 3:10). One of the main reasons for the Exodus narrative was, I believe, the historical opportunity for the Hebrew God to reveal Himself as more powerful than the Egyptian gods. In other words, the great "I AM" not only wanted to deliver His people from the Egyptian bondage, but He wanted to "execute judgment" against "all the gods of Egypt" (Exod. 12:12). Numbers 33:4 says, "For the Egyptians buried all their firstborn, which the Lord had smitten among them: upon their gods also the Lord executed judgments."

Thus Yahweh manifested his superiority over Osiris, Isis, Pharaoh, and the various other gods assigned to protect the famous Egyptians. Dr. Jones says, "It would be a mistake to overlook the fact that, taken individually, each plague of the Exodus stands alone as a specific judgment of a particular Egyptian god; while, viewed collectively,

the plagues of the Exodus illustrate God's supremacy over, and his attitude toward, the corpo-
rate sphere of the gods of mythology."

The Plagues of Exodus

Let's consider a brief overview of the plagues
of the Exodus, and their respective condemna-
tions of the Egyptian gods.

1. The Nile Plague

> And the Lord spake unto Moses, Say unto
> Aaron, Take thy rod, and stretch out thine
> hand upon the waters of Egypt. . . . that they
> may become blood . . . and Moses and
> Aaron did so, as the Lord commanded;
> and he lifted up the rod, and smote the
> waters that were in the river, in the sight of
> Pharaoh, and in the sight of his servants;
> and all the waters that were in the river
> were turned to blood. (Exod. 7:19-20)

Why would Yahweh turn the Nile into blood?
Because the Nile was worshiped as the single most
important element needed for the ongoing success
of the culture, economy, and paganism of the
Egyptian people. The annual flooding of the Nile
brought new life and sustenance to over 1,000
miles of Egyptian-dominated settlements, and the
watery event was perceived by the Egyptians as
the best evidence that the gods of the Nile were
pleased. When the Hebrew God challenged the
welfare and divinity of the Nile River, He was
striking a blow at the core of the Egyptian's faith
and pantheon.

First, the waters of the Nile were considered
sacred. Blood, on the other hand, was considered
an abhorrence to the Egyptian people. The Nile

River was supposedly protected from the contamination of human blood and other such impurities by the fearsome ram-headed god, Khnum, who consorted with Sati, the goddess of Elephantine, as the dispenser and protector of the cool waters. Secondly, the Nile was "possessed" by the spirit of Hapi, the son of Horus, who was often depicted as a corpulent man with the breasts of a female (representing the abundance and succoring of the Nile) and was honored as the god who, through using the silt and waters of the Nile, provided the abundant fertility of the land of Egypt. At other times, Hapi was depicted as a mummified man with the head of a baboon, a portrayal in which he was considered the guardian of the lungs of the deceased and the Nile-servant of Osiris. Keeping Osiris happy was important to the welfare of the Nile, because the origin of the Nile was not known in ancient times (the central African location was not discovered until 1862) and the Nile's origin was considered by the Egyptians to be the spiritual bloodstream, or divine "life flow," of the netherworld, Osiris. Turning the Nile into blood was thus, in part, a mockery of the Osiris blood-myth by the Hebrew God, Yahweh. Thirdly, the fish of the Nile were considered sacred and were supposedly protected by two powerful goddesses— Hathor, the goddess of the sky and the queen of heaven (who protected the *chromis* or "small fish"), and Neith, the very ancient goddess of war who protected the *lates* (large fish), which were also considered to be her children. Neith was a powerful Egyptian deity, the sister of Isis, and the protectress of Duamutef, the god who watched over the inner stomach of the dead. More importantly, she was the mother of the Nile-god Sobek, an evil god with the head of a crocodile, to whom pharaoh may have "offered" the Hebrew male children when he commanded the midwives to throw them into the Nile. (Exod. 1:22)

Another Nile crocodile god, Apepi, was the arch rival of the sun god Ra, and may have been one of the "serpents" who appeared before Pharaoh and Moses in Exodus 7:10-12. We read, "And . . . Aaron cast down his rod before Pharaoh . . . and it became a serpent (tanniym, dragon or crocodile) . . . the magicians of Egypt, they also did in like manner with their enchantments . . . and they became serpents [*crocodiles*, Sobek and Apepi?]: but Aaron's rod swallowed up their rods." Since the word *tanniym* is not translated "serpent" anywhere else in Scripture, Dr. Jones believes, as do many other Bible scholars, that *tanniym* should be interpreted as dragons or "crocodiles" in the Book of Exodus, as it was thus translated throughout the Books of Isaiah and Ezekiel. Either way, by turning the Nile River into blood, no less than nine separate deities were judged by the Hebrew God and found to be inferior and under His authority; the Nile River, Khnum, Sati, Hapi, Osiris, Hathor, Neith, Sobek, and Apepi. Through the first plague Yahweh confirmed that He alone is the supplier of every human need, and the true Judge of the after life and only Sovereign of destiny.

2. The Frog Plague

> And the Lord spake unto Moses, Go unto Pharaoh, and say unto him, Thus saith the Lord, Let my people go. . . . And if thou

refuse to let them go, behold, I will smite all thy borders with frogs: And the river shall bring forth frogs abundantly. . . . And Aaron stretched out his hand over the waters of Egypt; and the frogs came up, and covered the land of Egypt. (Exod. 8:1-3; 6)

When I was a young Christian I had an interesting experience during a time of intercessory prayer. I was fasting and praying for the salvation of a member of my wife's family when suddenly the image of a frog appeared in my mind's eye. The vision startled me, because it was unexpected and powerful. No matter how I tried, I could not shake the uncanny feeling that a "frog" was resisting my prayer. It had the appearance of a typical river frog, but it stared at me as if to warn me that I had wandered into its territory and that it was fully intending to defend its position within the life of the person for whom I was praying. After a while, it became obvious that whatever or whomever the frog creature was, it was not going away, so I rebuked it "in the name of Jesus," and it immediately vanished! Some time later, I was amazed to discover that certain demons can appear as images of frogs. In the Book of Revelation, we read: "And I saw three unclean spirits like frogs come out of the mouth of the dragon, and out of the mouth of the beast, and out of the mouth of the false prophet" (Rev. 16:13). My experience had been genuine, and, over time, helped me to understand that the Hebrew depiction of frogs as unclean animals was perhaps based on an ancient and spiritual revelation from Yahweh.

To the ancient Egyptians, however, frogs were sacred animals, and, ultimately, the infants of the frog-goddess Heka. Heka played an important role in the development of infants, including humans, beginning at the embryonic stage and continuing up until childbirth. She was, thus, an important patroness of midwives and a powerful goddess of fertility. As the wife of Khnum, she assisted in the original creation of mankind and was closely associated with Hapi, who held the divine frog in his hands as the waters of nourishment flowed from her mouth.

When the *krur* (frogs) increased along the banks of the river during the annual receding of the Nile, it was perceived by the Egyptians as a good Heka omen. It's easy to see how the Plague of the Frogs was a substantial embarrassment to the Egyptians, to have the frog-goddess babies so multiplied that one could not walk upon the ground or move within the house without squashing the divine creatures beneath their feet. Pharaoh could not order the Hebrew slaves to destroy and haul the frogs away, as it was a capital offence to kill a frog in Egypt! How powerful the Hebrew Creator-God must have appeared, compared to the stupidity and stench of the creator-frog goddess, as her infants lay rotting in massive filthy heaps, covering nearly every square inch of Pharaoh's Egyptian empire. Through the plague of the frogs, the mystical power (in the chapter on Greece we shall discuss how Heka was associated with Hekate, the Greek goddess of mysticism and witchcraft) of Heka was reduced to nothing more than a greasy pavement crushed to death beneath the feet of the sorrowful Egyptians.

3. Plague of Lice

And the Lord said unto Moses, Say unto Aaron, Stretch out thy rod, and smite the dust of the land, that it may become lice throughout all the land of Egypt. And they did so; for Aaron stretched out his hand with his rod, and smote the dust of the earth, and it became lice in man, and in beast; all the dust of the land became lice throughout all the land of Egypt. (Exod. 8:16-17)

Four distinct facts stand out in the plague of the lice: First, the priests of Egypt were immaculate regarding their purifications. Discovering a single louse would have rendered an Egyptian priest unclean, and, as such, incapable of ministering in the temple. The shutdown of the priestly ministry would have been no small matter, as the priesthood numbered in the thousands of men who maintained a strict regimen of daily ministering, bathing, shaving, and sacred purification. Such priests exercised great influence over the common Egyptians, and were considered the uppermost servants of the gods, the "consecrated ones" who carried out the required daily ceremonies of the hundreds of Egyptian temples deemed necessary for the ongoing functionality of the local community. The religious duties of the priests included two main categories: 1) carrying about the little shrines or oracles (small replica temples containing statues of the gods) which were made available to the common people (those who could not enter beyond the veil); and, 2) performing the mystery rituals in the inner sanctums or "holy of holies" of the temples. The difference between the two priestly categories was that the portable gods were publicly available to nod their heads and speak (it's been suggested that the priests spoke for the idols while moving their mouths with a string) while the mystery functions of the priesthood were highly secretive and included the important creation rituals conducted in the inner sanctums of the main temples, like those of Amun-Ra at Karnak, where a priestess known as the "hand of god" performed ritual masturbations on the priests as a form of imitative magic (referring to the Atum masturbation/creation myth). This practice was considered necessary for the ongoing balance of nature, the annual flooding of the Nile, and regulating the seasons.

Moses was a man "learned in [such] wisdom of the Egyptians" (Acts 7:22). As such, he was aware of, and may have been trained in, the mysteries of the Egyptian priesthood. It's even possible that Moses served as an Egyptian priest. The name Moses means to be "drawn out of" or "born of" and was usually associated with a priestly Egyptian deity, i.e., Thothmoses (born of Thoth), Amenmosis (born of Amen), or Rameses (born of Ra). The slight variations of the spelling of Moses (mosis, meses, etc.) did not change the priestly Egyptian meaning. This has caused some scholars to conclude that the Hebrew Moses may have been named after a Nile deity by the Pharaoh's daughter (Exodus 2:10), and that he served as an Egyptian priest who later dropped his Nile deity-name reference upon encountering the omnipotent Yahweh, the God of his fathers. Whether or not that's true, Moses was raised in the Pharaoh's court, thus he had a special understanding of the far-reaching ramifications of the plague of the lice. Moses understood that when every micro-particle of dust began to crawl upon the Egyptians, the priesthood was ceremonially unclean, and thus immobilized. The masturbation mysteries of Karnak could not be performed. The portable gods could not walk and talk. The seasons could not bring forth their blessings. While this kind of reasoning may seem simplistic, such imitative magic, as performed by the Egyptian priesthood, was central to the Egyptian way of life and was considered of the highest importance.

The second point of interest concerning the plague of the lice involves the fact that Pharaoh was supposedly the incarnation of Horus and the son of the Sun god Ra. He was, thus, god incarnate. The dust of Egypt was, therefore, holy ground. To say the least, it was a serious slap in Pharaoh's face for the Hebrew God to transform the sacred dust of Ra into lice.

The third notable point concerning the plague of the lice is that the magicians (priests) of Egypt could not duplicate the miracle, as they had duplicated the first two plagues. The Hebrew God was perhaps illustrating that He alone has the ability to create life out of the dust of the earth. Even the magicians testified, "This is the finger of God" (Exodus 8:19).

Fourth, Geb (earth) was the god who protected the soil, while Seth was, among other things, the angry god of the desert sand. In the Osiris myth, it was Seth who raged against the other gods in his bid to become the greatest among the Egyptian pantheon. In the plague of the lice, Yahweh was perhaps mocking the Egyptian religion by causing

the dust god, Seth, to literally struggle against
Geb, Ra, and Osiris, while leaving the Egyptians
to suffer as collateral casualties.

4. Plague of Flies

> And the Lord said unto Moses, Rise up
> early in the morning, and stand before
> Pharaoh . . . and say unto him, Thus saith
> the Lord. . . . if thou wilt not let my people
> go, behold, I will send swarms of flies upon
> thee, and upon thy servants, and upon thy
> people, and into thy houses. . . . and the
> Lord did so; and there came a grievous
> swarm of flies . . . and. . . . the land was
> corrupted [destroyed] by reason of the
> swarm of flies. (Exodus 8:20-24).

The beetle was known in Egypt as a fly. The
scarab beetle was the sacred emblem of the sun
god Ra and was the symbol of eternal life. But the
flies of the forth plague were most likely a blood-
sucking breed that spread blindness and disease
among the populace that lived along the Nile.
Whereas such flies were generally disliked by the
Egyptians, they were, nevertheless, revered as the
servants (demons?) of Vatchit, the Egyptian "lord
of the flies." In this context, it's possible that the
Hebrew God was administering a threefold
judgement: first, of the Egyptians for their
veneration of the fly-deities; second, of the sun
god Ra, the Egyptian almighty creator; and third,
of Vatchit himself, the Egyptian equivalent of
Baalzebub (Beelzebub), the ancient god who,
according to various eastern religions, was the evil
god and "lord of the flies."

The name Baalzebub originally derived from
two different words: *Baal* (lord, master), and *zebub*

(of flies). While the original meaning is unclear, and may have referred to a certain priestly interpretation of the flight path of flies as an oracular communication between a Baal and his followers, some have pointed out that flies are present at decaying bodies, and thus Baal-zebub may have been a kind of Baal-Osiris; a lord-demon of the human corpse.

According to the *Grimorium Verum* and the *Grand Grimoire* (18th century textbooks on magic), Baalzebub manifested himself in the image of a huge fly whenever he was summoned by the sorcerer.[2] Whether Baalzebub, like Vatchit, commanded the flies to do his bidding, or delivered from their nuisance, is unclear. Additionally, since the title "Baal" referred to any lord, deity, or human master, there were many gods of antiquity known as a Baal; i.e. Baal-berith (lord of the covenant), Baal-Gad (lord of the fortune), Baal-hazor (lord of the village), and so on. That some Baals were worshiped by the Egyptians is known from the titles of certain Egyptian provinces; i.e. Baal-ze-phon ("Baal-of-the-North" or "Hidden Place") of Exodus 14:2. In times of great distress, it was usually a Baal that was called upon for help, and people who sought material prosperity believed their lives could be improved by offering their firstborn child as a sacrifice to the deity. The Greek author Kleitarchos recorded the dastardly process of sacrificing infants to Baal three hundred years before Christ:

> Out of reverence for Kronos [Baal], the Phoeniciens, and especially the Carthaginians, whenever they sought to obtain some great favor, vowed one of their

children, burning it as a sacrifice to the deity, if they were especially eager to gain success. There stands in their midst a bronze statue of Kronos, its hands extended over a bronze brazier, the flames of which engulf the child. When the flames fall on the body, the limbs contract and the open mouth seems almost to be laughing [such areas of child sacrifice were often called "the place of laughing"], until the contracted body slips quietly into the brazier.

The sacrifice of babies to Baal was widespread in antiquity and was practiced by the children of Israel under the reign of King Ahab and Queen Jezebel. A recent archeological find illustrated how far-reaching such offerings were. It unearthed the remains of over 20,000 infants who had been sacrificed to a single Baal. Ahaziah, King of Israel, may have authorized such a child sacrifice when he sent messengers to the Philistine city of Ekron to inquire of the fly-god whether he (the king) would recover from his illness. Yahweh intervened and instructed Elijah to prophesy to the King:

> Thus saith the Lord, Forasmuch as thou hast sent messengers to inquire of Baalzebub the god of Ekron, is it not because there is no God in Israel to inquire of his word? Therefore thou shalt not come down off that bed on which thou art gone up, but shall surely die. (2 Kings 1:16)

The Hebrews acknowledged Baalzebub as Satan's highest power and often referred to him as Beelzeboul, "lord of the height," a classification in which he was depicted as the dark atmospheric god who controlled the cosmos, or circumambient "air." Baalzebub eventually developed into a demon-god of such evil reputation that he became known as "the prince of devils" (Matt. 12:24). Milton referred to Baalzebub in *Paradise Lost* as Satan's chief lieutenant, and, in the litanies of the witches' Sabbath, Baalzebub is ranked, together with Lucifer and Leviathan, as an equal member of the supreme trinity of evil. The mocking of Vatchit, as the Egyptian equivalent of Baalzebub, and, thus, as the ultimate manifestation of evil, may have been what the Hebrew God had in mind during the plague of the flies.

5. The Deadly Murrain

> Then the Lord said unto Moses, Go in unto Pharaoh, and tell him, Thus saith the Lord God of the Hebrews, Let my people go, that they may serve me. For if thou refuse to let them go. . . . Behold, the hand of the Lord is upon thy cattle which is in the field. . . . there shall be a very grievous murrain. (Exodus 9:1-3)

The first chapter showed how, down through the ages, Satan distorted the various aspects of the Original Revelation of God. The sacred Apis bull of Egypt was a perfect example of such plagiarism in that the Apis bull was a demonization of the life of Jesus, especially of the protoevangelium, the biblical promise of an immaculately born Son of God, who would also be God in flesh. (See Gen. 3:15; Isa. 7:14) Cattle, and especially the Apis bull, were sacred to the Egyptians. But the Apis bull (also known as Serapis or Osorapis) was special in that it was supposedly born of a miraculous conception when, every twenty-five years, divine moonlight (or lightning) struck a cow and it con-

ceived. The Apis bull was thus considered to be
the incarnation of god on earth. During its life
span, the Apis was worshipped as both the son,
and incarnation, of Ptah, the Universal Architect
god. As Ptah incarnate, the Apis embodied the
Egyptian logos god who created, according to a
later version of the Egyptian creation myth (the
Memphite cosmology), all of creation by the authority of his spoken word. In death the Apis
supposedly experienced a "resurrection" with
Osiris, and thus the Apis bull, identified with Osiris,
was a remarkable parallel of the Christian Messiah.

For practical reasons, the Apis bull was, for the
most part, kept in seclusion. The Egyptian priests
cared for the sacred animal and worked with a
team of doctors and nutritionists in maintaining
the bull's health. At the end of the twenty-five year
cycle, a new bull was chosen with the pomp and
ceremony of royalty. A celebration followed the
selection and, for a period of forty days thereafter, the Egyptian women raised their dresses and
exposed themselves to the bull. Such exposure
was thought to capture the fertility energies of the
Apis, and to excite the life-giving waters of Osiris.
It was also believed that a special generational
blessing came upon the exposed women's offspring. At the end of the forty days of "exposure,"
the new bull was removed to the Apis temple in
Memphis where it was kept in a special sanctuary.
It was thereafter publicly displayed during special
occasions only. We find the Apis sanctuary mentioned in, *The Geography of Strabo* (63 B.C., A.D. 26):

> Memphis itself, the royal residence of the
> Aegyptians [Egyptians], is also near

Babylon; for the distance to it from the Delta is only three schoeni. It contains temples, one of which is that of Apis, who is the same as Osiris; it is here that the bull Apis is kept in a kind of sanctuary, being regarded, as I have said, as god.[3]

Once the new Apis was inaugurated, the old bull was drowned, mummified, mourned, and placed into a huge sarcophagus. The burial rites of the passing bull were so revered and costly that they were paralleled in Egypt only by those of the Pharaoh. The comprehensive nature of such Apis burial rituals was illustrated in 1851, when 60 Apis sarcophagi of red and black granite weighing more than 60 tons each were discovered in Saqquara, just west of Memphis, where the Apis temple stood. I once took notes on, and photographed, the mummified head of one such bull. It was obvious from the detail and craftmanship, that great reverence was given to the animal during the mummification process. Especially impressive were the elaborate glass eyes that had been placed into the eye sockets, and the golden sun-disk of Ra that rested between the horns. Such golden discs were similar to the moon-discs worn by other members of the divine bovine family, including those donned by Hathor, the cow-goddess-mother of the sun god, Ra. While other religions have practiced similar veneration of cattle, most notably Hinduism in India where the humped Zebu cow continues to be worshipped as the respresentative of Aditi, the "sinless cow," nowhere was the deification of such animals more noteworthy than in Egypt.

The ancient Egyptians considered all cattle to be sacred sources of generative power, and the

Sekhmet, by Brooke Townsend

cults of Apis and of Hathor thus set the standards of eastern myth and ritual. This fact has caused the plague of the deadly murrain to be considered an especially effective grievance, as, in a single move, it repudiated the six most important aspects of the Apis cult: 1) it devastated the protected livestock of the Egyptians including the vast herds of Pharaoh; 2) it illustrated God's unlimited power when, miraculously, none of the Hebrew cattle died; 3) it humiliated the Universal Architect god, Ptah, and exposed him as a helpless demon; 4) it destroyed the dominion of the sacred Apis and Mnevis bulls of Heliopolis; 5) it judged the goddess Hathor, and the god Osiris, and found them to be inferior; and 6) it nullified the generational blessings of Apis-Osiris (Serapis). Amazingly, after all of this evidence, the foolish heart of Pharaoh was hardened against the Hebrew God.

6) The Plague of Boils

> And the Lord said unto Moses and unto Aaron, Take to you handfuls of ashes of the furnace, and let Moses sprinkle it toward the heaven in the sight of Pharaoh. And it shall become small dust in all the land of Egypt, and shall be a boil breaking forth with blains upon man, and upon beast, throughout all the land of Egypt. (Exod. 9:8-9)

During the third Egyptian Dynasty, at least 1,000 years before the Exodus, a man named Imhotep served as the vizier of the Pharaoh Zoser. Imhotep was an engineering genius and built the first-known massive stone structures, including the great Step-Pyramid (still standing) at Saqquara.

From history, we learn that Imhotep's well-founded distinction as a builder was surpassed only by his talent as a skilled magician and healer. When the Egyptians suffered under a seven-year famine that occurred during the reign of Zoser, the king appealed to Imhotep, who in turn consulted the sacred books.

After several days, Imhotep emerged from isolation and announced to the king "the hidden wonders, the way to which had been shown to no king for unimaginable ages." Zoser, impressed with Imhotep's discernment, obeyed the divinations. Simultaneously, Egypt withdrew from the famine and Imhotep was decreed the chief Kheri-heb priest ("son of Ptah") of Egypt. But the popularity of Imhotep's life eventually gave way to the fame that followed his death, as, later he was elevated, deified, and transformed into a healing god. By the time of the reign of the Pharaoh Menkaure (B.C. 2600), temples throughout Egypt were dedicated to the god Imhotep. Such temples contained incubation or "sleeping" chambers used in the convalescence of the sick and the mentally diseased, and the same became acknowledged as the most potent healing alchemies of Egypt. The incubation-temple of Imhotep at Memphis, for instance, proved to be so popular that the Greeks identified Imhotep with Asclepius, the Greek god of healing, and affirmed his divine membership within the powerful Egyptian "trinity" composed of Imhotep, Ptah, and Sekhmet the lion-headed goddess.

It's said that Imhotep convinced the Egyptians that premature forms of sickness and disease could be ultimately avoided if the proper aspects of healing-magic were carefully employed. The magicians of Imhotep used the magic crystals and incantations of Isis to call upon Sekhmet, the goddess-sovereign of epidemics and diseases, to work with the positive energies of Serapis in the administration of the healing needs of the Egyptians. Such rituals were often accompanied by burnt offerings (sometimes human), and the ashes of the same were sprinkled into the air as a health-blessing for the Egyptians. At other times, the diagnosis called for an extended stay in the temple of Serapis where the sick or injured person was placed under the mystical spell of the katoche. Such katoche supposedly provided the internal coercion of the god and ultimately led to the proper diagnosis, and divine assimilation, of the transmissible and healing energies of the god. The katoche, affiliated with Imhotep's sleep-wizardry, was linked to the mystical crystals of Isis. These, in turn, were joined with Sekhmet's administration of the overall life-giving energies of Ptah and Osiris. Combined, they provided the Egyptian magicians with the powerful and esoteric tools necessary for the overall health (?) of the people. Such magic was, indeed, powerful, and the fame of such men and magic (Jannes and Jambres) continued up until the time of the New Testament (2 Tim. 3:8).

When the Hebrew God attacked the divine health of the Egyptians by placing a filthy, eruptive disease of boils upon the population, He accomplished what no other surrounding power had attempted to do: 1) He sent the respected Egyptian magicians fleeing, powerless, before Moses—unclean and unable to perform their priestly duties; 2) He illustrated the inferiority of

Seth, by Brooke Townsend

the Egyptian high gods, Ptah and Osiris, and denounced them as helpless demons; 3) He judged the lion-headed goddess Sekhmet and demonstrated her impotence at regulating diseases; 4) He altered the ritual of "casting ashes" and made the ashes a curse instead of a blessing; and 5) He mocked the temples of Imhotep and Serapis, and, thereby, notified the surrounding nations that neither crystals, nor psychic dreams, nor positive energies, nor coercions of men and their gods, can defy the incontestable will of Yahweh.

7) The Plague of Hail

> And the Lord said unto Moses. . . . Behold, tomorrow about this time I will cause it to rain a very grievous hail, such as hath not been in Egypt since the foundation thereof even until now. . . . So there was hail, and fire mingled with the hail, very grievous. . . . And the hail smote throughout all the land of Egypt all that was in the field, both man and beast; and the hail smote every herb of the field, and brake every tree of the field. (Exodus 9:13; 18; 23-25)

The goddess Nut was the Egyptian protectress of the sky and weather, and was depicted in Egyptian art as a woman arched over the earth, with the stars above her back and the earth (her brother Geb) beneath her belly. She was the consort of Osiris, the "blesser" of crops and fertility, and was cherished as the caring mother "sky-goddess" by the agricultural people of the Fertile Crescent. According to myth, Nut elevated herself each morning upon her fingers and toes and thereby

provided an expanse between herself and Geb/
earth. The spherical covering generated by Nut's
towering action allowed the sun god Amun-Ra to
coat the earth with light, and the warmth of the
new day was received as a blessing of the goddess.
At night, when Nut lay down, the expanse closed
anew, and darkness covered the earth. To the
Egyptians, this was the natural order of things.
But when violent storms erupted and the daytime
skies were darkened, the same was perceived as a
disturbance in the original cosmic scheme.

Nut was displeased with such nonconforming
weather, and, at times, the skies grew red with the
blood of her wounds (other myths define the red
skies as Nut's menstrual period) as she struggled
against the storm to restore the cosmic rhythm.
For the sake of her people, the Egyptians, Nut
bravely fought to maintain the essential universal
cycle. Both men and gods depended on the cycle
of Nut. Amun-Ra needed her expanse to visit the
earth each day. Seth needed the same to dry the
desert sand. Osiris needed Nut's meteorological
blessings to sustain the agriculture; and Pharaoh
desired the sanctions of Nut for two essential
reasons: first, she controlled the atmospheric
conditions surrounding the Pharaoh's Egyptian
empire, and second, she conquered the fierce
storms that could herald the death of a king. For
these and other reasons, Nut was particularly
important to Egyptian devotions.

When the Hebrew God sent a storm of hail
and fire "such as there was none like it in all the
land of Egypt since it became a nation" (Exodus
9:24), He was repudiating the combined efforts of
Nut, Geb, Amun-Ra, Osiris, and Pharaoh, to con-

trol the atmospheric conditions that befell the land of Egypt. A similar storm of fire mingled with hail is predicted to hit the earth again during the Great Tribulation. We read, "The first angel sounded, and there followed hail and fire mingled with blood, and they were cast upon the earth" (Rev. 8:7). Just as Pharaoh rejected Yahweh, embraced pagan idols, and hardened his foolish heart, modern men seem destined to repeat the same mistakes. We find "the rest of the men which were not killed by these plagues yet repented not of the works of their hands, that they should not worship devils, and idols of gold, and silver, and brass, and stone, and of wood" (Rev. 9:20). Such verses indicate a latter-day revival of idolatry, and provide the impetus for the last two chapters of this book, in which we discuss the prophetic and extensive aspects of modern paganism.

8) The Plague of Locusts

> Thus saith the Lord God of the Hebrews. . . . if thou refuse to let my people go, behold, tomorrow will I bring the locusts into thy coast: And they shall cover the face of the earth, that one cannot be able to see the earth: and they shall eat the residue of that which is escaped, which remaineth unto you from the hail, and shall eat every tree which groweth for you out of the field. (Exodus 10:3-5)

The locust plague was an awesome spectacle and was one of the most feared pestilences of the ancient world. Such invasions darken the sky and destroy every green thing. An average locust can consume its weight in food daily, and can quickly amass an army of insects numbering in the hundreds of millions per square mile. In 1927, a few African locusts were spotted near a river in Timbuktu. Within three years, the whole of west Africa was besieged by the creatures. Eventually, locusts covered an area more than 2,000 miles wide—extending from Ethiopia and the Belgian Congo to the luxuriant farm lands of Angola. Finally, 14 years after the plague began, 5,000,000 square miles of Africa (an area twice the size of the United States!) had been destroyed by the locusts.

In ancient times, the idea of such a calamity brought instant terror to the hearts of the vegetation-dependent Egyptians. To avoid defoliation created by Edipoda locusts and other living things, the Egyptians prayed to Sobek—the crocodile-headed god of animals and insects. As the son of Neith, Sobek was the underworld demon of the four elements (fire, earth, water, and air). At his cult center in Arsinoe (Crocodilopolis), where devotees cared for his sacred crocodiles, Sobek was ritually associated with Ra (fire), Geb (earth), Osiris (water), and Shu (air). It was believed that Sobek controlled such elements to the extent that he restrained the activity of certain creatures within specific habitats. Thus, Sobek limited the activity of a crocodile within water, a locust within air, etc. His mastery of such elements was demonstrated in the Isis/Osiris myth, when Isis searched the Nile for the severed body-parts of her husband/brother Osiris. Sobek, out of respect for the goddess, limited the appetite of the river animals, and thus spared the floating pieces of Osiris.

As an Egyptian demon, Sobek was associated with the goddess Ammit—the crocodile-headed

Sobek, by Brooke Townsend

"eater of souls" that dwelt beneath the Scales of Justice in the judgment hall of Osiris. At other times, Sobek and Ammit were depicted as one and the same. In his book, *Egypt, Gift of the Nile*, Walter A. Fairservis, Jr. paraphrased a section of the *Book of the Dead*. In the following paragraph he describes Sobek in the role of Ammit:

> According to the book Meri would at last reach the place of the greatest test of all—the Great Judgment Hall. Here in the presence of Osiris, King of the Dead, Anubis the embalmer, Thoth the ibis-headed scribe, and the forty-two gods of judgment, the heart of Meri would be placed on the scales to be weighed with the "Feather of Truth." If Meri had been a bad man in life, no words or deeds could save him now. His heart would not balance the Feather of Truth, and Meri would be thrown to Sebek (Sobek), the crocodile-headed eater of souls.[4]

In another Sobek-related chapter of the *Book of the Dead*, "Making The Transformation Into The Crocodile-God," we read:

> The Osiris Ani, whose word is truth, saith:-
> I am the crocodile god [Sobek] who dwelleth amid his terrors. I am the Crocodile-god and I seize [my prey] like a ravening beast. I am the great Fish which is in Kamui. I am the lord to whom bowings and prostrations are made in Sekhem.

Such prostrations were made to Sobek along the Nile river and at his centers at Kom Ombo and Thebes. Sobek's oblations often included human sacrifices, and this may have been the

Pharaoh's intention when he commanded the mid-wives to throw the Hebrew children into the Nile. The offerings anticipated Sobek's favor in delivering from bothersome insects, and, if a person wanted to eradicate an annoyance, such as locusts, he or she simply made supplications to Sobek while chanting, "To Sobek with it (the locust)!" The modern-day slang, "to Hell with it!" is a derivative of such a ritual.

It was undoubtedly against the demon-god Sobek, and his pestilence-protection rituals, that the Hebrew God initiated the relentless plague of the locusts. In so doing, Yahweh revealed that Sobek was unable to control the elements, or limit the activity of God's insect army. Sobek's companion, the high god Ra (of fire), could not scorch the creatures. Ra's son Shu, the Egyptian god of sun and wind (air), could not blow the consuming insects away.

It was not until the Hebrew God commanded "a mighty strong west wind, which took the locusts, and cast them into the Red sea" (Exod. 10:19), that the grievous plague was ended. Even so, the heart of Pharaoh was hardened against the God of Israel.

9) The Plague of Darkness

> And the Lord said unto Moses, Stretch out thine hand toward heaven, that there may be darkness over the land of Egypt, even darkness which may be felt. And Moses stretched forth his hand toward heaven; and there was thick darkness in all the land of Egypt three days: They saw not one another, neither rose any from his place for three days: but all the children of Israel had light in their dwellings. (Exodus 10:21-23)

My research companion, Dr. Jones (I call him "Indy" after Indiana Jones), spoke recently of his trek through Hezekiah's Tunnel in Jerusalem. He described the interior of the cave as dominated by a darkness "that could be felt, compounded by feelings of claustrophobia, obscurity, and utter dejection." One can imagine the terrors that the Egyptians must have experienced when the Hebrew God devised a darkness that spread throughout "all the land of Egypt" and lasted for three days! Such an occurrence must have caused an unparalleled despondency, and most certainly would have devastated the Egyptian's religious idea that Amun-Ra ("The Hidden One") was the incarnation of the midday sun, and the most powerful god in the Cosmos.

The Egyptians referred to Amun-Ra as "the king of the gods." They believed that no deity was superior to him, and that the whole of the pantheon would perish without his symmetry. The sun itself was considered "the Eye of Amun-Ra," and the light and warmth of the midday sun was perceived as the bath of his blessing. Amun-Ra was also called Khepri (the rising sun), and Atum (the setting sun), so that each position of the sun, rising, midday, and setting, was perceived as a posture of Amun-Ra. According to myth, Amun-Ra, like the Sumerian god "Utu" (Shamash), traversed the sky each day. At night, he journeyed through the underworld where the evil god Apepi attempted to prevent him from rising again. With the assistance of the magical masturbation rituals conducted by the Egyptian priests, Amun-Ra was empowered each night to conquer Apepi and become the Ra-Harachte, the bright and morning sun. His cult center at Thebes was the primary location of such rituals, and the same site boasted the largest religious structure ever built, the temple of Amun-Ra at Karnak. Interestingly, the great Temple of Amun-Ra (with its 100 miles of walls and gardens) was the primary object of fascination and worship by the nemesis of Moses, the Pharaoh of the Exodus, Ramses II. It was believed that each pharaoh, including Ramses II (who completed Amun-Ra's temple), reconciled his divinity in the company of Amun-Ra during the festival of Opet. The festival was held at the Temple of Luxor and included a procession of gods carried on barges up the Nile river from Karnak to the Temple. The royal family accompanied the gods on boats while the Egyptian laity walked along the shore, calling aloud and making requests of the gods. Once at Luxor, the Pharaoh and his entourage entered the holy of holies where the king joined his *Ka* (the mysterious ritual is unknown) and transmogrified into a living deity. Outside, large groups of dancers and musicians waited anxiously. When the king emerged "transformed" (supposedly), the crowd erupted in gaiety. From that day forward Egypt was "guarded" by their king and the Pharaoh was considered the son of the sun god—the earthly representative of the creator deity, Amun-Ra.

Subsequently, it was believed that the midday sun arose above Egypt because the Pharaoh had been honored and inaugurated in the Temple of Amun-Ra. If the sun was ever darkened or eclipsed, it was an evil omen for the king. Egypt's priests carefully interpreted such "signs," and even offered life-saving maneuvers to the Pharaoh. But, when

three days of utter darkness paralyzed the
Egyptians (Exodus 10:21-23), the number three
being understood by the Hebrews and the
Egyptians as representing divine providence, the
king's magicians were uncharacteristically silent.
Like the three hours of darkness that accompanied
the death of Christ (Luke 23:44), the sovereignty
of the Highest was believed to be at work. It would
do no good to call upon the goddess Nut. She had
been proven to be powerless before Yahweh. If
the God of the Hebrews was at work, Nut could do
nothing to elevate herself nor could she force the
light of Amun-Ra to come forth. The sky-cow-
goddess Hathor had been equally humiliated by
Israel's Lord during the deadly murrain, and the
evil god Sobek had been found impotent at
controlling the element of sky. The mystical spells
of Isis were useless against Yahweh. The priestly
magic, paralyzed, and now, Amun-Ra, the Creator
"king of the gods" and champion of the Egyptian
pantheon, was confirmed helpless before the God
of Hebrew slaves. "And Pharaoh called unto Moses,
and said. . . . Get thee from me, take heed to
thyself, see my face no more; for in that day thou
seest my face thou shalt die. And Moses said, Thou
has spoken well, I will see thy face again no more"
(Exodus 10:24; 28-29). With this final act, Pharaoh
sealed the destiny of his kingdom, and, sadly, his
firstborn son.

10) Death of the Firstborn

> And Moses said, Thus saith the Lord, About
> midnight will I go out into the midst of
> Egypt: And all the firstborn in the land of
> Egypt shall die, from the firstborn of Pha-
> raoh that sitteth upon his throne, even unto

the firstborn of the maidservant that is behind the mill; and all the firstborn of beasts.
(Exodus 11:4-5)

At least six deities were committed to the
protection of Egypt's children. They included
Heka, the mystical frog-goddess, who oversaw the
development of animals and children beginning
at the embryonic stage; Isis, the advocate-mother
of the children who kept her word; Min, the god
of virility who conferred reproductive vigor upon
men and who was ritually called upon to produce
an heir to the pharaoh; Horus, the son of Isis and
Osiris, who protected the Pharaoh's son; Bes, the
patron protector of mothers and their children;
and the Pharaoh himself—Egypt's protector-
incarnation of Amun-Ra and Horus. The female
deities, Heka and Isis, oversaw different aspects of
the children's physical development, while Min
and Horus were the powerful male deities
responsible for the spiritual progress and overall
health of the child.

Min's full name was Menu-ka-mut-f ("Min, Bull
of his Mother"), and he was often worshiped in
the image of a white bull. At other times, Min was
depicted as a bearded man with an oversized
phallus. Such iconography of Min served to verify
his position as the eminent Egyptian god of male
sexuality, while also accounting for his mythological
marriage to Qetesh' the equivalent Egyptian deity
of female sexuality. Egyptian boys supposedly
acquired their sexual strength from Min, and
subsequently made offerings of lettuce (considered
an aphrodisiac by the Egyptians) to this god. The
Greeks confused Min with Pan, the Dionystic god
of unbridled sexual desire, and thus participated

in the orgiastic festivals held in his honor. But the
most important area of Min's dominion, insofar as
the Pharaoh was concerned, was the mystical
relationship between the god and the royal family,
including Min's association with the princely heir
of Egypt, the pharaoh's son. The pharaoh was so
concerned with the blessings of Min that he
ceremoniously hoed the lettuce fields during the
festival of this god. The idea was to humble himself
in the presence of Min and thereby procure divine
favor and reproductive synergy. Sexual energy,
such as was abundantly produced by Min, was
believed to be synonymous with health and
longevity. Thus, if the pharaoh and his son were
to live long and prosperous lives, they required
the favor of Min, the preeminent god of sexual
power. Such power of Min would have likely been
sought during the death of Egypt's firstborn.

Legend has it that the god Horus was also
involved in guarding the pharaoh's son, due, in
part, to the mythology that the child Horus had
been subjected to homosexual rape by the evil
god Seth. The adult Horus was, thus, protective of
children in general. Equally important, Horus was
believed to incarnate himself within the living
pharaoh, and to fill the heart of the pharaoh with
respect for the father. The virtue of such parental
respect was an important part of ancestor ritual,
and referred to the story of Horus and his war
with evil Seth over the murder of his father. Such
myths supposedly contributed to the survival of
the pharaoh and his son in two important ways: 1)
Horus was the protector of the father and child,
and perched above and behind the pharaoh,
spreading his wings around and guarding the

pharaoh's head (another plagiarism reminiscent of the Old Testament passage "in the shadow of Thy wings"); and 2) Horus reminded the royal son of his responsibilities toward the father, especially of the offerings to be made daily at the deceased father's tomb. Such offerings were deemed necessary for maintenance in the afterlife, and amulets (the eye of Horus) placed beside the offerings protected the stomach of the dead. In this way, the living pharaoh (Horus) served the needs of the deceased father, while the predecessor pharaoh conducted himself as the Osiris in the underworld.

In the classic film by Cecil B. DeMille, *The Ten Commandments*, Yul Brynner, in the role of the pharaoh, placed his firstborn son in the arms of the falcon-headed god, Seker (who protected the dead as they passed through the underworld), and said, "Seker, great lord of the lower world, I . . . bow before you now. Show that you have power above the God of Moses. Restore the life he has taken from my son. Guide back his soul across the lake of death to the place of living men." Ramses II undoubtedly prayed in such fashion for the life of his son. Nevertheless, "at midnight the Lord smote all the firstborn in the land of Egypt, from the firstborn of Pharaoh who sat on his throne unto the firstborn of the captive who was in the dungeon" (Exodus 12:29).

By initiating the death of the firstborn, Yahweh executed His final judgment "against all the gods of Egypt" (Exodus 12:12). Heka was proven powerless. Isis was defunct. Min was unable to energize the pharaoh's son. Horus was equally inept. The pharaoh was without a successor to watch over his tomb. Amun-Ra was without earthly representation. Egypt was without an heir. and the whole of the Egyptian pantheon, with its magic, myths, and rituals, crumbled at once beneath the feet of the Hebrew God. "And Pharaoh rose up in the night, he, and all his servants . . . for there was not a house where there was not one dead. And he called for Moses and Aaron by night, and said, Rise up, and get you forth from among my people, both ye and the children of Israel; and go, serve the Lord, as ye have said" (Exod. 12:30-31).

Important Notes
Regarding the Gods of Egypt

The following notes on the Egyptian deities are important and relate to the last two chapters of the book.

From the example of Amun-Ra we learn: 1) prehistoric Egyptians believed in the same idea that evolutionists subscribe to today—the premise that the oceans preceded and in some way contributed to life on earth; 2) Amun-Ra was a self-existing primordial earth spirit; 3) Amun-Ra was associated with moisture spirits (Shu and Tefnut); 4) sacred prostitution was practiced at the Temple of Amun-Ra as a form of imitative magic; 5) the Eye of Amun-Ra (the sun) was considered a living part of "god"; and 6) the Egyptians treated nature "properly" in order to maintain the blessings of the nature spirits.

From the example of Geb we learn: 1) Geb was the original Egyptian "Father Earth"; 2) his sister/wife Nut was the original Egyptian "Mother Sky"; 3) the earth and sky spirits are the "parents" of humanity; and 4) it is important to care for the earth and sky if we want their ongoing blessings.

From the examples of Osiris and Isis we learn: 1) Osiris was the original Egyptian lord of the dead; 2) the Egyptians believed in a netherworld judgement; 3) the Egyptians believed in the *Ka*, an invisible duplicate body throughout life and provided the person with a new body in the underworld; 4) the goddess Isis was the undisputed Queen of magic; 5) her spells were necessary for the navigation of this world and the afterlife; 6) the magic of Isis, if performed properly (at the right time of the day, with the proper crystals and words) would have the effect of altering reality, manipulating the laws of physics, and forcing the being or object to which they were directed into compliance; 7) sacred prostitution (magic sex) was practiced at the temples of Isis and Osiris as a form of imitative magic; 8) imitative magic extended into the spirit world (i.e., placing a wooden crocodile at the grave of an enemy would produce a real crocodile in the underworld); 9) the Egyptians had numerous oracles, and practiced divining through amulets and crystals; 10) the Egyptians practiced self-healing through psychic dreaming, crystals, and positive energies which were assimilated at the temples of Imhotep; and 11) the Egyptian religion may have started following an encounter with the "Watchers," a powerful group of fallen angels who visited the earth during antiquity.

From the example of the Plagues of the Exodus we learn: 1) the plagues of the Exodus illustrate God's supremacy over, and His attitude toward, idolatry and paganism; 2) similar plagues are forecast for the Great Tribulation (boils, hail, darkness, locusts, etc.), and, like the plagues of the Exodus, they will be directed at paganism (see Rev. 9:20); 3) Egyptians, like modern pagans, worshiped natural phenomena such as rivers, trees, etc., and attributed divine characteristics to such; 4) the Egyptians treated the earth with respect and believed that, if they did so, she (the earth) would continue the cycle of seasons; 5) the magicians of Egypt were powerful and could mimic many of the miracles of God; 6) the creatures of the Nile (fish, hippos, etc.) were sacred, and, like the environmental movement today, were often placed above the needs of the community; 7) Egyptians, like modern abortionists, often protected sacred animals while sacrificing children; 8) gods (demons) could manifest themselves through animal forms; and 9) the following deities were among those directly impacted by the Plagues of the Exodus: Ammit, Amun-Ra, Apepi, Apis, Geb, Hapi, Hathor, Heka, Horus, Imhotep, Isis, Khnum, Min, Neith, Nile River, Nut, Osiris, Pharaoh, Ptah, Sati, Seker, Sekhmet, Seth, Serapis, Shu, Sobek, Tefnut, and Vatchit.

Notes

1. Will Durant, *The Story of Civilization* (New York: Simon and Shuster, 1996), vol. 1, 199.

2. Richard Cavendish, *Man, Myth & Magic* (Italy: B.P.C. Publishing Ltd., 1970), vol. 2, 237.

3. Horace Leonard Jones, *The Geography of Strabo* (Cambridge, MA: Harvard University Press, 1967) vol. 8, 2453.

4. Walter A. Fairservis, Jr., *Egypt, Gift of the Nile* (New York: The Macmillan Company), 115.

The Gods Who Walked among the Greeks

"Mother, what the gods send us, we mortals bear perforce, although we suffer; for they are much stronger than we."
—The Homeric Hymns

The Dorians came from out of the north by the tens of thousands. They were nearly invincible Indo-European invaders riding in horse-drawn chariots of war. Between B.C. 2800 and 2000, they conquered most of the indigenous inhabitants of the Middle East, from the inland people of Asia Minor to the Macedonians and beyond, and they did it in the name of their sky god, the thunderous and fearsome Zeus. They came, they conquered, and finally they forged a new and curious fusion of pagan theologies, of the Dorians, Myceneans, and Minoans, into a new and influential society of gods known as the Olympians. Later, known as the famous (and sometimes infamous) gods of Greece, these powerful deities dwelt together above the towering Mount of Olympus in the north, where they "spent their delightful days." Under Zeus, the greatest of the Olympian gods, was Hera, Poseidon, Hades, Demeter, Apollo,

Artemis, Ares, Aphrodite, Hermes, Athene, Hephaestus, and Hestia (later replaced by Dionysus). Simultaneously, a complex system of lesser Greek deities developed beneath the principle Olympian gods including Adonis, Selene, Hypnos, Asclepius, Eros, and, of course, Hercules.

The Major Oracle Gods— Zeus and Apollo

In Hesiod's *Theogony* we are told of a time when twelve pre-Olympian gods, known as the Titans, ruled the Universe. These were the children of Mother Earth (Gaia), who gave birth to the "elder" gods by cohabiting with Uranus (Heaven), who also sired the mountains, the sea, the hundred-handed monsters, and the Cyclops. The important Titans included Oceanus, Tethys, Mnemosyne, Themis, Hyperion, Lapetus, and Atlas. But when Uranus attempted to imprison the Titans within the body of his wife (the earth), Cronus, "the youngest and most terrible of her children," conspired with his mother and castrated Uranus with a sickle. The mutilation of Uranus separated Heaven from Earth and succeeded in freeing the Titans. When the powerful Cronus later cast the severed genitals of his father into the sea, a white foam enveloped them, from which Aphrodite was born; thus, the name Aphros, or "foam-born."

As the newly-crowned king of the gods, Cronus took note of the beauty of his sister Rhea, and married her. Six famous god-children were born of their union: Hestia, Demeter, Hera, Hades, Poseidon, and Zeus. Since Mother Earth and Father Uranus warned Cronus that his offspring would someday try to overthrow and replace him as the king of the gods, Cronus attempted to circumvent the possibility by swallowing each child whole as it was born. But Rhea, "cunning as the night air," replaced the baby Zeus with a cloth-wrapped stone which Cronus unwittingly swallowed instead. Afterward, Rhea hid the young Zeus at Crete, where he was fed on the milk of the goat Amalthaea and where he remained until adulthood, protected by the nymphs. Years later, Zeus somehow forced Cronus to regurgitate his brothers and sisters. A fierce ten-year war ensued, and the younger and powerful Olympian gods overthrew the older Titans, casting them down into Tartarus (Hell) where they (except for Hecate) were to remain fettered forever.

Eventually, Zeus reconciled with the Titans and proclaimed Cronus the ruler of the Golden Age. But, for the time being, Zeus, fresh from the triumphant victory, summoned his brothers, Hades and Poseidon, and decreed that the universe should thereafter be divided among them. They cast lots, and the sky became the dominion of Zeus; Poseidon was chosen to rule over the sea, and the inner-earth or underworld was declared the haunt of Hades. Notwithstanding, the surface of the earth was determined to be neutral territory, a place where sky, sea, and the underworld joined together, and thus a place where any of the gods could rest, chiefly upon Mount Olympus. Hephaestus was commissioned, and immediately adorned the heavenly stronghold of Olympus with intimate dwelling-places for the victorious gods, each surrounding the beautiful palace of Zeus.

Then, according to a former vow, Zeus be-

Zeus, by Brooke Townsend

stowed additional privileges upon the Olympians. It seems that Zeus had vowed to his supporters that victory over Cronus and the Titans would result in "spheres of influence" for each of the faithful gods. Consequently, Hephaestus was made the "lord of the fire." Demeter was given the dominion of agriculture. Artemis was placed over the wild animals. Hera, the wife of Zeus, was made the overseer of the various phases of female life. Hermes became the messenger of Zeus and the protector of travellers. Apollo was placed over music, prophecy, healing, and so on. Even so, Zeus remained the preferred god of the early Greeks.

There was scarcely any part of the Greek's daily life in which Zeus was not involved. He was Zeus Herkeios (protector of the house) and Zeus Ktesios ("the Acquirer"). He was Zeus Hikesios (friend of the fugitive) and Zeus Polieus (guardian of the city). His firmly-held position as the supreme and high god within the Greek religion has been easily verified by archaeology, including the discovery of the great temple of Zeus. This masterwork stood in the southern part of the precinct of Zeus at Olympia (the Atlis), and exhibited the famous gold and ivory colossus of Zeus by Pheidias (destroyed in A.D. 462), a single masterpiece estimated to be the greatest work of art in all of antiquity, and one of the Seven Wonders of the ancient world.[1]

More important in ritual than in mythology, was the oracle and altar worship that developed throughout Asia Minor in response to the popularity of Zeus. In Pergamum, perpetual sacrifices were offered to the deity upon the

towering and famous 40 foot high altar of Zeus,
the same artifact which now stands inside the Berlin
Museum. Some scholars believe that Antipas, the
first leader and martyr of the early Christian church
in Pergamum, was slain for resisting the altar
worship of Zeus in Pergamum. Tradition holds
that Antipas was slowly roasted to death inside the
statue of a bull, the symbol and companion of
Zeus, and some claim that the passage in
Revelation 2:13 is a reference to the cult worship
of Zeus at Pergamum. We read: "I know thy works,
and where thou dwellest, even where Satan's seat
is. . . . wherein Antipas was my faithful martyr, who
was slain among you, where Satan dwelleth."
Others believe this passage refers to Caesar
worship, while still others (myself included)
contend that the phrase in Revelation 2:13 is a
reference to the cult worship of Asclepius, the
Greek god of healing. But the argument could be
made for a Pergamum connection between Zeus
and the biblical Satan, as both were considered
gods of thunder, Zeus in antiquity and Satan in
modern times. Zeus was also known as the king or
"prince" of the air, as was Satan. (See Eph. 2:2)

Lastly, altars have been discovered near
Pergamum which were dedicated to Zeus
Kataibates, which most accurately means "Zeus who
descends" (in thunder and lightning), and, of
course, Jesus said of Satan, "I beheld Satan as
lightning fall [descend] from heaven" (Luke 10:18).
In any case, the fact that Zeus was a powerful
presence in ancient cult and ritual is undisputed.
His principle oracle was at Dodona, the chief city
of Epirus and the "land of the oak trees," where
a shrine to Zeus had existed since the second

Aphrodite, by Brooke Townsend

millennium B.C. For a while, the oracle at Dodona
rivaled Apollo's famous oracle at Delphi, as con-
sultations with Zeus grew in popularity. At Dodona,
Zeus provided the inquiring mortals with divine
guidance by whispering through the leaves of a
sacred oak tree attended to by bare-footed priests
called Selloi.[2] At other times, Zeus communicated
through the splashing of water in a nearby sacred
spring, or through the cooing of sacred pigeons.
Eventually, his answers were simplified and divination came through the casting of lots or by interpreting the echo of a gong. But it was the oak-
tree oracle at Dodona that claimed to be the oldest in Greece and the "father of gods and men."

The connection between Zeus and the tree
oracles probably began with certain prehistoric
religious ideas from Crete and undoubtedly refers
to the earliest marriage of the Dorian Zeus and
the Minoan/Cretan willow goddesses. In Hagia
Triada, Zeus was called Zeus Welkhanos, which
means the "god of the willow-tree."[3] He was also
known by the name Welkhanos at Gortyna and at
Phaistus where he was somehow ritually associated
with his lover Leto. The cult worship of Zeus and
Leto in Phaistus was curious in its own right, because it connected the ancient elements of earth
worship (the children of Gaia conversing through
various nature manifestations, i.e., the willow-tree)
and transsexualism. In fact, the worship of Zeus
was sometimes overshadowed in Phaistus by the
cult of Leto, as the Cretan youths cast off their
boyish garments during their initiation into man-
hood. The festival was called the *Ekdysai* ("Casting
off") and was associated with the myth of
Leucippus, a peculiar legend in which a baby girl

(Leucippus) was born to a woman named Galatea who preferred instead to have a son, so she persuaded Leto to let the girl change her sex into a boy when she grew up. During the Cretan initiation, the young men apparently lay down beside a statue of Leucippus in the temple of Leto where the blessings of growth and of fertility could be invoked. Comparable traces of transsexuality, lesbianism, witchcraft, and feminism, were incorporated into various other goddess myths and will be considered later in this book.

Apollo and the Pythians

According to the Greeks, the greatest outcome of the love affair between Zeus and Leto was the birth of the most beloved of the oracle gods, Apollo. More than any other god in classical Greece, Apollo inspired the nobler passions of poetry, painting, and music. He was the god of prophecy, music, archery, and healing. But the primitive deity whose myth grew into the Olympian Apollo was probably of a much lower original stature as some histories suggest that Apollo started out as a Hittite wolf god who was venerated by shepherds and who protected the flocks against the ravages of wild animals. The Hittite people called him Apulunas or Appaliunaas. The more liberal Greek scholars agreed with the pre-Olympian origin of Apollo, and some even claimed that he had been the god of the Hyperboreans, an ancient and legendary people to the north. Herodotus claimed that the Hyperboreans continued in their worship of Apollo even after his induction into the Greek pantheon, and that they made an annual pilgrimage to the land of Delos where they participated in the famous Greek festivals of Apollo.

Lycia, a small country in southwest Turkey, also had an early connection with Apollo, and he was known there as Lykeios, which some have adjoined to the Greek Lykos or "wolf," thus, the ancient title: "the wolf slayer." But, in the end, it was the mythology of the Greeks that secured Apollo's place in history. Apollo, with his twin sister Artemis, was said by the Greeks to have been born in the land of Delos, the children of Zeus and of the Titaness Leto. Appropriately, an important oracle existed at Delos and played a significant role in the festivals of the god.

While the Delos oracle was important, it was nevertheless the famous oracle at Delphi that became the popular mouthpiece of the Olympian. Located on the mainland of Greece, the omphalos of Delphi (the stone which the Greeks believed marked the center of the earth) can still be found among the ruins of Apollo's Delphic temple. On a singular column was carved the three maxims: "Know thyself," "Nothing in excess," and "Go surety, and ruin is at hand." So important was Apollo's oracle at Delphi that wherever Hellenism existed, its citizens and kings, including some from as far away as Spain, ordered their lives, colonies, and wars, by its sacred communications.

At Delphi, the Olympian gods spoke to mortal men through a priesthood, which interpreted the trance-induced utterances of the Pythoness or Pythia. She was a middle-aged woman who sat on a copper-and-gold tripod, or, much earlier, on the "rock of the sibyl" (medium), and crouched over a fire while inhaling the smoke of burning

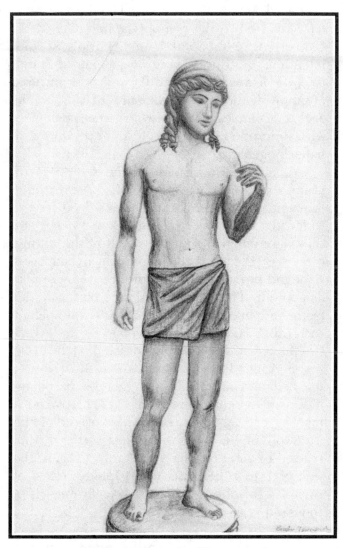

Apollo, by Brooke Townsend

laurel leaves, barley, marijuana, and oil, until a sufficient intoxication for her prophecies had been produced. While the use of the laurel leaves may have referred to the nymph Daphne (Greek for Laurel), who escaped from Apollo's sexual intentions by transforming herself into a laurel tree, the leaves also served the practical purpose of supplying the necessary amounts of hydrocyanic acid and complex alkaloids which, when combined with hemp, created cerebral and powerful hallucinogenic visions.

An alternative version of the Oracle myth claims that the pythia sat over a fissure breathing in magic vapors that rose up from a deep crevice within the earth. The vapors "became magic" as they were mingled with the smells of the rotting carcass of the dragon Python, which had been slain and thrown down into the crevice by Apollo as a youth. The former version is obviously the truth, and, in either case, it was under the spell of such drugs (and spiritual forces?) that the Pythia prophesied in an unfamiliar voice thought to be that of Apollo himself. During the pythian trance, the medium's personality often changed, becoming melancholic, defiant, or animal-like. This psychosis may have been a source for the origin of the werewolf myth, or lycanthropy, as the Pythia reacted to an encounter with Apollo/Lykeios, the wolf god. In either case, the Delphic "women of python" prophesied in this way for nearly a thousand years and were considered to be a vital part of the religious order, and of the local economy, of every Hellenistic community. An interesting example of this is found in the New Testament Book of Acts:

> And it came to pass, as we went to prayer,
> a certain damsel possessed with a spirit of
> divination [of python, a seeress of Delphi]
> met us, which brought her masters much
> gain by soothsaying: The same followed
> Paul and us, and cried, saying, These men
> are the servants of the most high God, which
> shew unto us the way of salvation. And this
> did she many days. But Paul, being grieved,
> turned and said to the spirit, I command
> thee in the name of Jesus Christ to come
> out of her. And he came out the same hour.
> And when her masters saw that the hope of
> their gains was gone, they caught Paul and
> Silas. . . . And brought them to the magis-
> trates, saying, These men, being Jews, do
> exceedingly trouble our city. (Acts 16:16-
> 20)

The story in Acts is interesting because it illustrates the level of culture and economy that had
been built around the oracle worship of Apollo. It
cost the average Athenian more than two days'
wages for an oracular inquiry, and a lawmaker or
military official seeking important State information was charged ten times that rate. That's one
reason the actions of the woman in Acts are difficult to understand. She undoubtedly understood
the damage that Paul's preaching could do to her
industry.

Furthermore, the Pythia of Delphi had a historically unfriendly relationship with the Jews and
was considered an enemy of the truth and a pawn
of demonic power by both the Jews and the Christians. Quoting again from *Spiritual Warfare—The
Invisible Invasion,*

Delphi with its surrounding area, in which
the famous oracle ordained and approved
the worship of Asclepius, was earlier known
by the name Pytho, a chief city of Phocis.
In Greek mythology, Python, the name-
sake of the city of Pytho, was the great
serpent or demon who dwelt in the mountains of Parnassus, menacing the area as
the chief guardian of the famous oracle at
Delphi. . . . In Acts 16:16, the demonic
woman who troubled Paul was possessed
with a spirit of divination. In Greek this
means a spirit of python (a seeress of
Delphi, a pythoness) . . . [and] reflects . . . the
accepted Jewish belief . . . that the worship
of Asclepius [Apollo's son] and other such
idolatries were, as Paul would later articu-
late in 1 Corinthians 10:20, the worship of
demons.[4]

It could be said that the Pythia of Acts 16
simply prophesied the inevitable. That is, the spirit
that possessed her may have known that the time
of Apollo's darkness was coming to an end, and
the spread of Christianity would ultimately lead to
the demise of the Delphic oracle. This is possible.
Demons are sometimes aware of changing dispen-
sations (compare the please of the demons in
Matthew 8:29, "What have we to do with thee,
Jesus, thou Son of God? art thou come hither to
torment us before the time?").

Perhaps the ancient spirit of Delphi understood the dispensation timing and power of the
gospel Paul was preaching? The last recorded
utterance of the oracle at Delphi seems to indicate
the spirit of the Olympians understood time for

domination was over. From *Man, Myth & Magic,*
we read:

> Apollo.... delivered his last oracle in the
> year 362 A.D., to the physician of the Em-
> peror Julian, the Byzantine ruler who tried
> to restore paganism after Christianity had
> become the official religion of the Byzan-
> tine Empire. "Tell the King," said the
> oracle, "that the curiously built temple has
> fallen to the ground, that bright Apollo no
> longer has a roof over his head, or pro-
> phetic laurel, or babbling spring. Yes, even
> the murmuring water has dried up."[5]

As the oracle at Delphi slowly diminished,
Apollo secured his final and most durable characterization through the influence of his favorite
son, Asclepius. Beginning at Thessaly and spreading throughout the whole of Asia Minor, the cult
of Asclepius, the Greek god of healing, became
the chief competitor of early Christianity. Asclepius
was even believed by many pagan converts of
Christianity to be a living (evil?) presence who
possessed the power of healing. Major shrines were
erected to Asclepius at Epidaurus and at
Pergamum, and for a long time he enjoyed a strong
cult following in Rome where he was known as
Aesculapius. Usually depicted in Greek and Roman art as carrying a sacred snake wound around
a pole, Asclepius was often accompanied by
Telesphoros, the Greek god of convalescence. He
was credited with healing a variety of incurable
diseases, including raising a man from the dead,
a miracle that later caused Hades to complain to
Zeus, who responded by killing Asclepius with a
thunderbolt. When Apollo argued that his son

had done nothing worthy of death, Zeus repented and restored Asclepius to life, immortalizing him as the god of medicine.

Because the snake was sacred to Asclepius and played a vital role in the healing rituals at his shrines (hospitals), some claim the healing cult of Asclepius began with the biblical story of Moses and the brazen serpent. We read: "And the Lord said unto Moses, Make thee a fiery serpent, and set it upon a pole: and it shall come to pass, that every one that is bitten, when he looketh upon it, shall live [be healed]" (Num. 21:8). In 2 Kings 18:4, the children of Israel developed a cult following of the brazen serpent and worshipped the image as a healing oracle. Some scholars believe the Greeks borrowed from this history in formulating the myth of Asclepius. Either way, Asclepius represented the last popular cult of the Olympian Apollo myths and was one of the most durable challenges to Christianity by the ancient pagan's who dominated Asia Minor for more than 4,000 years. So popular had the iconography of Asclepius become that, to this day, the sacred snakes of the healing god can be found adorning the entry doors and halls of hospitals in cities around the world.

Facts about Dionysus (Bacchus)— The Mystery God

Dionysus, the Thirteenth God of the Greeks, was the divine son of Zeus and of the mortal Semele. He was often depicted as the inventor of wine, abandon, and revelry, but this description seems inadequate in that it refers only to the basic elements of intoxication and enthusiasm, which were used by the Bacchae (the female participants of the Dionystic mysteries; also known as Maenads and Bacchantes) in their rituals to experience Dionysus, the intoxicating god of unbridled human desire. Followers of Dionysus considered him to be much more than the inventor of wine. He was the presence that is otherwise defined as the craving within man that longs to "let itself go" and to give itself over to the baser earthly desires. What a Christian might resist as the lustful desires of the carnal man, the followers of Dionysus embraced as the incarnate power that would, in the next life, liberate the souls of mankind from the constraints of this present world, and from the customs which sought to define respectability through a person's obedience to moral law.

Until that liberating (?) day arrived, the worshippers of Dionysus attempted to bring themselves into union with the god through a ritual casting off of the bonds of sexual denial and primal constraint by seeking to attain to a higher state of ecstasy. The uninhibited rituals of ecstasy (Greek for "outside the body") supposedly brought the followers of Dionysus into a supernatural condition that enabled them to escape the temporary limitations of the body and mind, and to achieve a state of enthousiasmos, or, "outside the body and inside the god." In this sense, Dionysus represented a dichotomy within the Greek religion, as the primary maxim of the Greek culture was one of moderation, or, "nothing too extreme." But Dionysus embodied the absolute extreme in that he sought to inflame the forbidden passions of human desire. Interestingly, as most students of psychology will understand, this gave Dionysus a stronger allure among the Greeks who otherwise tried in so many ways to suppress and control the wild and secret lusts of the human heart. But Dionysus resisted every such effort, and, according to myth, visited a terrible madness upon those who tried to deny him his free expression. The Dionystic idea of mental disease resulting from the suppression of secret inner desires, especially aberrant sexual desires, was later reflected in the atheistic teachings of Sigmund Freud. Thus, Freudianism might be called the grandchild of the cult of Dionysus.

Conversely, the person who gave himself over to the will of Dionysus was rewarded with unlimited psychological and physical delights. Such mythical systems of mental punishments and physical rewards based on resistance and/or submission to Dionysus, were both symbolically and literally illustrated in the cult rituals of the Bacchae, as the Bacchae women (married and unmarried Greek women had the "right" to participate in the mysteries of Dionysus) migrated in frenzied hillside groups, dressed transvestite in fawn skins and accompanied by screaming, music, dancing, and licentious behavior. When, for instance, a baby animal was too young and lacking in instinct to sense the danger and run away from the revelers, it was picked up and suckled by nursing mothers who participated in the hillside rituals. But when older animals sought to escape the marauding Bacchae, they were considered "resistant" to the will of Dionysus and were torn apart and eaten alive as a part of the fevered ritual.

Human participants were sometimes subjected to the same orgiastic cruelty, as the rule of the cult was "anything goes," including lesbianism,

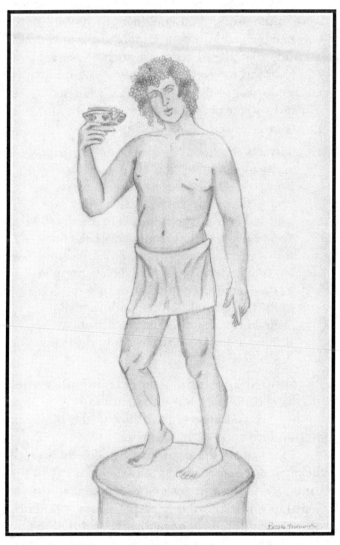

Dionysus, by Brooke Townsend

bestiality, etc. Later versions of the ritual
(Bacchanalia) expanded to include pedophilia and
male revelers, and perversions of sexual behavior
were often worse between men than they were
between men and women. Any creature (sometimes
a child) that dared to resist such perversion of
Dionysus was subjected to sparagmos ("torn apart')
and omophagia ("consumed raw"). In B.C. 410,
Euripides wrote of the bloody rituals of the Bacchae
in his famous play, *The Bacchantes:*[6]

> The Bacchantes. . . . with hands that bore
> no weapon of steel, attack our cattle as they
> browsed. Then wouldst thou have seen
> Agave mastering some sleek lowing calf,
> while others rent the heifers limb from limb.
> Before thy eyes there would have been hurl-
> ing of ribs and hoofs this way and that, and
> strips of flesh, all blood be-dabbled, dripped
> as they hung from the pine branches. Wild
> bulls, that glared but now with rage along
> their horns, found themselves tripped up,
> dragged down to earth by countless maid-
> ens hands.

Euripedes went on to describe how Pentheus,
the King of Thebes, was torn apart and eaten alive
by his own mother as, according to the play, she
fell under the spell of Dionysus.

The tearing apart and eating alive of a sacrificial victim may refer to the earliest history of the
cult of Dionysus. An ancient and violent cult ritual
existing since the dawn of paganism stipulated
that, by eating alive, or by drinking the blood, of
an enemy or an animal, a person might somehow
capture the essence or "soul-strength" of the victim. The earliest Norwegian huntsmen believed

this, and they drank the blood of bears in an effort to capture their physical strength. East African Masai warriors also practiced omophagia, and sought to gain the strength of the wild by drinking the blood of lions. Human victims were treated this way by Arabs before Mohammed, and head-hunters of the East Indies practiced omophagia in an effort to capture the essence of their enemies.

Today, omophagia is practiced by certain Voodoo sects as well as by cult Satanists. It should be pointed out that such modern omophagia illustrates a continuing effort on the part of Satan to distort the original revelations of God. Eating human flesh and drinking human blood as an attempt to "become one" with the devoured is, in many cases, a demonization of the Eucharist, or Holy Communion. But sparagmos and omophagia, as practiced by the followers of Dionysus, was not an attempt of transubstantiation (as in the Catholic Eucharist), nor of consubstantiation (as in the Lutheran communion), nor yet of a symbolic ordinance (as in the fundamentalist denomination), all of which have as a common goal—the elevating of the worshipper into a sacramental communion with God. The goal of the Bacchae was the opposite: the frenzied dance, the thunderous song, the licentious behavior, the tearing apart and eating alive, all were efforts on the part of the Bacchae to capture the essence of the god (Dionyus) and bring him down into an incarnated rage within man. The idea was not one of holy communion, but of possession by the spirit of Dionysus. When one recalls the horrific rituals of the followers of Dionysus, it's easy to believe that a demonic possession actually occurred. A Christian should find this idea as plausible, and, it would seem, so did the Hebrews.

The Hebrew people considered Hades (the Greek god of the underworld) to be equal with Hell and/or the Devil, and many ancient writers likewise saw no difference between Hades (in this sense the Devil) and Dionysus. Euripedes echoed this sentiment in the Hecuba, and referred to the followers of Dionysus as the "Bacchants of Hades."[7] In Syracuse, Dionysus was known as Dionysus Morychos ("the dark one") a fiendish creature; roughly equivalent to the biblical Satan, who wore goatskins and dwelt in the regions of the underworld.[8] In the scholarly book, *Dionysus Myth and Cult,* Walter F. Otto connected Dionysus with the prince of the underworld. He wrote:

> The similarity and relationship which Dionysus has with the prince of the underworld (and this is revealed by a large number of comparisons) is not only confirmed by an authority of the first rank, but he says the two deities are actually the same. Heraclitus says, "Hades and Dionysus, for whom they go mad and rage, are one and the same."[9]

But the Hebrews considered the magic (witchcraft) of the Bacchae to be the best evidence of Dionysus' Satanic connection, and, while most of the details are no longer available because Dionysus was a mystery god and his rituals were revealed to the initiated only, the Hebrew prophet Ezekiel described the "magic bands" (kesatot) of the Bacchae, which, as in the omophagia, were used to capture (magically imprison) the souls of men. We read,

> Therefore, thus says the Lord GOD, "Behold I am against your magic bands [kesatot] by which you hunt lives [souls] there as birds, and I will tear them off your arms; and I will let them go, even those lives [souls] whom you hunt as birds." (Ezek. 13:20 NAS)

In Acts 17:34, we read of a soul liberated from the control of Dionysus: "Howbeit certain men clave unto [Paul], and believed: among the which was Dionysius the Areopagite." To carry the name of Dionysus usually meant one of two things: 1) the parents were devotees of Dionysus and thus the child was "predestined" to be a follower of the god; or 2) the individual was under the spell of the kesatot. The kesatot was a magic arm band used in connection with a container called the kiste.

Wherever the kiste is inscribed on sarcophagi and on Bacchic scenes, it is depicted as a sacred vessel (a soul prison?) with a snake peering through an open lid. How the magic worked and in what way a soul was imprisoned is still a mystery. Pan, the half-man/half-goat god (later relegated to devildom) is sometimes pictured as kicking the lid open and letting the snake (soul?) out. Such loose snakes were then depicted as being enslaved around the limbs, and bound in the hair, of the Bacchae women. Such imagery of Pan, the serpents, the imprisoned souls, and the magic Kesatot and Kiste, have not been adequately explained by any available authority, and the interpretation of them as a method for producing zombies is thus subject to ongoing scrutiny. Since the prophet Ezekiel spoke of the efforts of the Bacchae to mystically imprison the souls of men through the magic bands of Dionysus, and since Pan was most beloved of Dionysus, because of his pandemonium ("all the devils") which struck sudden panic in the hearts of men and beasts, and as the serpent was universally accepted by the Hebrews as a symbol of occult devotion, it can be easily surmised that the iconography of Dionysus represented the most tenacious effort on the part of the Bacchae to embrace the will of evil supernaturalism.

Facts about Demeter— The Mystery Goddess

While the mysteries of Dionysus were closely associated with those of Demeter (some very ancient histories suggest that Dionysus, Demeter, and Persephone were a type of unholy trinity), the rituals of Demeter, the goddess of agriculture and fertility, were different in that they were observed by married women only (participation was mandatory for all wives of Greek citizens), and, unlike the rituals of the Bacchae, chastity was strictly enforced. The Thesmophoria was the most popular of the fertility festivals held in honor of Demeter, and it drew the largest crowds at Athens and at Eleusis for nearly 2,000 years. Demeter's celebrations also boasted the most protected cult secrets of the mystery religions because her rituals were performed inside the inner sanctum of the Temple of Demeter (the Telesterion) and were so well-guarded by the Temple devotees that little has survived to enlighten us as to what actually occurred there. Only those portions of the Thesmophoria held outside of the Temple were publicly recorded (sparsely) and provide us with a partial historical record.

What is known is that the rituals of the Thesmophoria were based on the mythology of the abduction and rape of Persephone (Proserpina), and of Demeter's (Persephone's mother) subsequent actions in searching for her daughter. The cult's rituals are, therefore, interpreted according to the Demeter myth. The myth claimed that Hades, the dark god of the underworld, fell in love with beautiful Persephone. One day, as she plucked flowers in a grassy meadow, Hades swooped down in his chariot and dragged Persephone down into the underworld, where he forced her to become his bride. Above ground, Demeter was distraught by her daughter's disappearance, and she searched the earth in vain to find her. With the help of Helios and Hecate, Demeter finally discovered the truth of what happened, and, in her fury, she demanded that Hades release her daughter. When Hades refused, Demeter sent a horrific famine upon the earth. Plants dried up; Seeds refused to sprout, and the gods began to suffer from a lack of sacrifices. Finally, Zeus dispatched Hermes to intercede with the lord of the underworld, and, after a great debate, Hades agreed to release Persephone if she would eat a pomegranate seed.

What Persephone did not understand was that by eating the pomegranate seed in the mystical location of the underworld, a sort of divine symmetry was created that bonded Persephone with Hades. This ensured that the goddess would automatically return to the underworld for a third part of each year (in the winter), during which time the seeds of the ground would not grow. Persephone thus became the upperworld goddess of youth and happiness, and the underworld queen of the dead; a dual role depicting her as both good and evil. On earth, she was the goddess of the young and the friend of the nymphs who appeared in the blooming of the spring flowers (symbolizing her annual return from Hades), and in the underworld she was the dreaded wife of Hades and the Queen of the Darkness who controlled the fates of deceased men. The reenactment of such myth, the abduction and rape of Persephone, was central to the rituals of the Thesmophoria, and, as such, were key to interpreting the bits of information that are known.

The festival of the Thesmophoria, sometimes called the Eleusinian Mysteries, lasted from three to ten days. Each day of the festival had a different name and included specific rituals. A highlight of the festival was a procession from Athens to Eleusis which was led by a crowd of children known as Ephebi. The Ephebi assisted in carrying the hiera (sacred objects), and in pulling a statue of Dionysus as a boy (Iacchos), and finally in the ceremonial cleansing of the initiates (candidates of the mystery religion) in the sea. Upon arriving at Eleusis, the women organized the first day of the celebration (Anodos) by building temporary shelters and electing the leaders of the camp. On the second day (Nesteia), they initiated the Greater Mysteries which, according to myth, produced the cult's magical requests (a fertile harvest). Such mysteries included a parody of the abduction and rape of

Persephone, and the positioning of the female devotees upon the ground weeping (in the role of Demeter for her daughter) and fasting for the return of Persephone (the return of spring). The setting upon the ground and fasting was also intended to mystically transfer the "energies" of the women into the ground, and thus into the fall seeds.

Not surprisingly, the festival was held during the time of the fall planting, so as to nearly guarantee a positive response to the cult's magic. On the fifth day of the festival, the participants drank a special grain mixture called *kykeon* (a symbol of Persephone) in an attempt to assimilate the spirit of the goddess. The idea was to produce a blessing of fertility, both of the crops and of children. About this same time, certain women, called *Antleriai*, were cleansed in the sea and then sent down into the mountainside trenches to recover the sacrificial piglets and various other sacred objects that had been thrown down into the hillside canyons several days earlier. The sacred objects included dough replicas of snakes and of genitalia, which were burned, with the piglets and a grain-seed-mixture, as an offering to Demeter.

The reason for the casting of the piglets into the mountainside cliffs has been thoroughly debated and no single interpretation has emerged as the absolute authority. While several mystical representations can be made of the symbology, and the dough replicas are obviously fertility symbols, pigs' blood was sacred to the gods and, thus, the piglets are key to understanding the ritual. Greeks venerated pigs because of their uncanny ability to find, and unearth, underground items (roots, etc.). Some scholars conclude from this that the ritual casting of the pigs "into the deep" was a form of imitative magic based on the underworld myth of Persephone and Hades. That is to say, casting the piglets into the deep canyon trenches, and fetching them out again, represented the descent of Persephone into the underworld and her subsequent ascension back up to the surface of the earth. The piglets in the trenches may have also served the practical purpose of supplying a host (body) for Persephone to hide in until the *antleriai* could assist her (by retrieving the piglets) in her annual escape from the underworld. Burning the piglets later that night would, according to an ancient religious idea that fire passes the soul from one location to another, free the spirit of Persephone into the upperworld (compare the children sacrificed to Baal who "passed through the fire" from the physical world into the spiritual). This interpretation sounds reasonable and is considered by some to be true.

Since the New Testament informs us that pagan rituals, such as those performed in the Thesmophoria, were the worship of demons, "The things which the Gentiles sacrifice, they sacrifice to devils . . ." (1 Cor. 10:20), one wonders if a connection between the ritual casting of the piglets down into the deep canyon trenches (representing a descent into hell), and the biblical story of the Gadarene demoniac, existed.

In Luke, chapter Eight, we read:

> And they arrived at the country of the Gadarenes. . . . And when he [Jesus] went forth to land, there met him out of the city a certain man, which had devils. . . . When

> he [the demoniac] saw Jesus, he cried out,
> and fell down before him, and with a loud
> voice said, "What have I to do with thee,
> Jesus, thou Son of God most high? I be-
> seech thee, torment me not". . . . And Jesus
> asked him, saying, "What is thy name?"
> And he said, "Legion:" because many dev-
> ils were entered into him. And they be-
> sought him that he would not command
> them to go out into the deep. And there
> was there an herd of swine feeding on the
> mountain: and they besought him that he
> would suffer them to enter into them. And
> he suffered them. Then went the devils out
> of the man, and entered into the swine:
> and the herd ran violently down a steep
> place into the sea, and were choked. (Luke
> 8:26-33)

The word *deep* in this text is *Abussos* (the Abyss),
and refers to the underworld, Bottomless Pit. Since
the principle elements of the sea, the swine, and
the deep were employed; and since the Abyss (part
of the underworld) was central to the narrative;
and since the cult rituals of the Thesmophoria
were well known throughout Asia Minor and were
considered by the Hebrews to be an activity of the
devil (the inhabitants of Hades were known as
"Demeter's people," and Hecate, the goddess of
witchcraft, was Perserphone's underworld guide
during the rituals); one could easily surmise that
Jesus was mocking the Thesmophoria. It is possible that Jesus was revealing, to His followers and
to the neighboring communities, that Dionysus
and Demeter were, in fact, devils. It may be a
stretch to suggest an interpretation of the biblical

story in this way, but clearly the similarities and historical proximities are startling, especially since the demons requested an entry into the swine.

Why would demons make such a plea? There are two possible connections with the Thesmophoria: 1) the demons believed that by entering the swine they could escape the under-world deep (as in the magical Persephone escape ritual described above); and 2) Jesus, by granting the request of the devils, was illustrating that the Thesmophoria ritual of casting the piglets into the deep was inherently demonic. Obviously, there are other possible interpretations of the narrative in Luke 8. But since this is the only record of Jesus granting the petition of demons, it seems possible that a powerful social commentary on a popular pagan idea, like that of the Thesmophoria of Demeter, was being made by the Master.

Demeter and the Mother Earth Spirit

While much is still unknown about the myster-ies of Demeter, the basis of her popularity was almost certainly rooted in her divinity as a mother-earth goddess. Demeter (De or Da "earth", and meter "mother") actually means "earth mother." As earth mother, Demeter was the giver of gener-osity and grace and the controller of the awesome forces of nature. She was loved as the giver of food and fertility and was feared as the taker of life. She could open her womb with blessings and abundance and could enclose the dead in her soil. Either way, at all times, she commanded absolute reverence.

Without a doubt, the worship of the earth's "spirit" as a mother, and the incarnation of the earth's fertility forces within specific goddesses, was one of the oldest and most widespread forms of paganism recorded in antiquity. Whether it was Inanna of the Sumerians, Ishtar of the Babylonians, or Fortuna of the Romans, every civilization had a sect of religion based on the embodiment of the earth's spirit as a mother-goddess. The Egyptians worshipped Hathor in this way, as did the Chinese, Shingmoo. The Germans worshipped Hertha as the great Earth Mother, and the apostate Jews idolized "the queen of heaven." In Greece, the queen of the Olympian goddesses and wife of Zeus was Hera, the benevolent earth mother. Before her was Gaia (Gaea, the Greek creator-mother earth) and beneath her were many other Greek earth goddesses, including Demeter, Artemis, Aphrodite, and Hecate.

The principal idea was, and evidently still is among New Age devotees, that the earth is a living entity. The ancient and universally accepted idea that the "living earth" was also a fertile mother was conceptualized in different ways and in various goddess myths and images throughout the ancient world. In *The Golden Asse,* by second century Roman philosopher Lucius Apuleius, evidence reveals that the spirit of the earth was perceived as a feminine force, and that such force incarnated itself at various times, and to different people, within the goddess mothers. Note how Lucius prays to the earth spirit:

> O blessed Queene of Heaven, whether thou be the Dame Ceres [Demeter] which art the original and motherly source of all fruitful things in earth, who after the finding of thy daughter Proserpina [Persephone],

through thy great joy which thou diddest
presently conceive, madest barrain and
unfruitful ground to be plowed and sowne,
and now thou inhabitest in the land of Eleusie
[Eleusis]; or whether thou be the celestiall
Venus . . . [or] horrible Proserpina . . . thou
hast the power to stoppe and put away the
invasion of the hags and ghoasts which
appeare unto men, and to keep them
downe in the closures [womb] of the earth;
thou which nourishest all the fruits of the
world by thy vigor and force; with whatso-
ever name is or fashion it is lawful to call
upon thee, I pray thee, to end my great
travaile.

The earth spirit responds to Lucius:

Behold Lucius I am come, thy weeping and
prayers hath mooved me to succour thee.
I am she that is the natural mother of all
things, mistresse and governesse of all the
elements, the initial progeny of worlds,
chiefe of powers divine, Queene of heaven,
the principall of the Gods celestiall, the
light of the goddesses: at my will the planets of the ayre [air], the wholesome winds
of the Seas, and the silence of hell be dis-
posed; my name, my divinity is adored
throughout all the world in divers man-
ners, in variable customes and in many
names, for the Phrygians call me the
mother of the Gods: the Athenians,
Minerva: the Cyprians, Venus: the
Candians, Diana: the Sicilians, Proserpina:
the Eleusians, Ceres: some Juno, other
Bellona, other Hecate: and principally the
aethiopians . . . Queene Isis.[10]

One could assume, based on such texts, that a single spiritual source (or realm) energized the many goddess myths. Likewise, in the ancient hymn, "To Earth, the Mother of All," Homer illustrates how the earth-spirit was universally involved in the affairs and lives of nations. Through Homer's dedication to the earth we discover how far-reaching and omnipresent the mother-earth spirit was thought to be:

> I will sing of well founded Earth, mother of all, eldest of all beings. She feeds all creatures that are in the world, all that go upon the goodly land, and all that are in the paths of the seas, and all that fly: all these are fed by her store. Through you, O queen, men are blessed in their children and blessed in their harvests, and to you it belongs to give means of life to mortal men and to take it away. Happy is the man whom you delight to honour! He hath all things abundantly: his fruitful land is laden with corn, his pastures are covered with cattle, and his house is filled with good things. Such men rule orderly in their cities of fair women: great riches and wealth follow them: their sons exult with ever-fresh delight, and their daughters in flower-laden bands play and skip merrily over the soft flowers of the field. Thus it is with those whom you honour O holy goddess, bountiful spirit. Hail, mother of the gods, wife of starry Heaven; freely bestow upon me for this my song substance that cheers the heart! And now I will remember you and another song also.[11]

From these and other ancient records, it is obvious that the earth was more than an agricultural or herbaceous facility to the pagans, she was the personable and "eldest of all beings," the "holy goddess," the "bountiful spirit," the all nourishing mother of men who manifested herself within the popular idols of the mother goddesses.

Christian theologians also believe the physical earth contains spiritual forces. In Revelation 9:14, we read of "the four angels which are bound in the great river Euphrates." Likewise, in Job 26:5, we find "Dead things are formed from under the waters." The literal Hebrew translation says, "The Rafa (fallen angels) are made to writhe from beneath the waters." Additional biblical references indicate the earth is a kind of holding tank, or prison, where God has bound certain fallen entities (2 Pet. 2:4; Jude 6). That such fallen spirits seek to communicate with, or participate in, the affairs of humanity, is described in Scripture. The Hebrew people were warned of spirits who seek regular communion with men (Deut. 18:11), and, when the witch of Endor communicated with the same spirits, they ascended up from "out of the earth" (1 Sam. 28:13). It would seem, based on such scriptures, that the dynamic or energy behind the earth-goddess-spirits is indeed real, and, according to the Christian doctrine, is identical with the legions of fallen spiritual forces that are bound within the earth and that seek association with men. Such conclusions can be made because of the obvious and physical location of the biblical demons within the body of the earth, and also because of the nature of the manifestations, or attributes, of the goddesses. As previously noted, the myths and rituals behind the earth-goddess-mothers, Isis, Demeter, and Persephone, were openly connected with the evil spirits of the un-derworld.

The Earth-Mother Hecate

Hecate, the Titan earth-mother of the wizards and witches, illustrates, perhaps better than any other goddess, the connection between the earth goddesses and the realm of evil supernaturalism. As the daughter of Perses and Asteria, Hecate (Hekate) was the only one of the Titans to remain free under Zeus. She was the mother of the wizard, Circe, and of the witch, Medea, and was considered to be the underworld sorceress of all that is demonic. This was because Hecate characterized the unknown night-terrors that roamed the abandoned and desolate highways. She was often depicted as a young maiden with three faces, each pointing in a different direction, a role in which she was the earth-spirit that haunted wherever three paths joined together. As the "goddess of three forms" she was Luna (the moon) in heaven, Diana (Artemis) on earth, and Hecate in the underworld. At times of evil magic, she appeared with hideous serpents, spreading demons, encouraging criminal activity, and revealing enigmatic secrets to the crones. At other times, she roamed the night with the souls of the dead, visible only to dogs, who howled as she approached. When the moon was covered in darkness, and the hell-hounds accompanied her to the path-beaten crossways, Hecate came suddenly upon the food offerings and dead bodies of murders and suicides that had been left for her by the fear-stricken common-folk. Her hounds bayed, the ghost-torches lit up the night, and the river nymphs

shrieked as Hecate carried away the mangled souls
of the suicides into the underworld caverns of
Thanatos (Death), where the shrill cries of such
damned-ones were known to occupy her presence.

As the dark goddess of witchcraft, Hecate, like
Isis, was worshiped with impure rites and magical
incantations. Her name was probably derived from
the ancient Egyptian word *Heka* ("sorcery" or
"magical"), which may explain her association with
the Egyptian frog goddess of the same name. This
may also explain the affiliation of frogs with witchcraft, and the various potions of frog-wart and
"hecateis" (Hecate's hallucinogenic plant, also
called Aconite), which supposedly sprouted from
the spittle of Cerberus (Hade's three-headed guard
dog), which fell to the ground when Hercules
forced him up to the surface of the earth.

Because her devotees practiced such magic
wherever three paths joined, Hecate became known
to the Romans as *Trivia* (tri "three," and via
"roads"). Later, when the Latin church fathers
compared the magic of the goddess Trivia with
the power of the Gospel, they found it to be
inferior, and the pursuit of Hecate's knowledge
became known as Trivial Pursuit, or inconse-
quential. But the fact that Hecate's followers
sincerely believed in, and feared, her magic and
presence, was legendary. We find an example of
such belief in the *Argonautica,* (Jason and the
Argonauts) by Apollonius Rhodius, when the
sorceress Medea provided a spell for Jason to use
in winning Hecate's assistance:

> Take heed now, that I may devise help for
> thee. When at thy coming my father has
> given thee the deadly teeth from the

dragon's jaws for sowing, then watch for the time when the night is parted in twain, then bathe in the stream of the tireless river, and alone, apart from others, clad in dusky raiment, dig a rounded pit; and therein slay a ewe, and sacrifice it whole, heaping high the pyre on the very edge of the pit. And propitiate only-begotten Hecate, daughter of Perses, pouring from a goblet the hive-stored labour of bees.

And then, when thou hast heedfully sought the grace of the goddess, retreat from the pyre; and let neither the sound of feet drive thee to turn back, nor the baying of hounds, lest haply thou shouldst maim all the rites and thyself fail to return duly to thy comrads." ... [and] Jason ... bathed his tender body reverently in the sacred river; and round him he placed a dark robe.... and ... he cut the throat of the sheep, and duly placed the carcase above; and he kindled the logs placing fire beneath, and poured over them mingled libations, calling on Hecate Brimo [the Mighty One] to aid him in the contests.

And when he had called on her he drew back; and she heard him, the dread goddess, from the uttermost depths and came to the sacrifice of Aeson's son [Jason]; and round her horrible serpents twined themselves among the oak boughs; and there was a gleam of countless torches; and sharply howled around her the hounds of hell. All the meadows trembled at her step; and the nymphs that haunt the marsh and the river shrieked, all who dance around

that mead of Amarantian Phasis. And fear
seized Aeson's son, but not even so did he
turn round as his feet bore him forth, till
he came back to his comrades.[12]

Such magic, as illustrated in the fiction above,
was employed by fearful men to appease Hecate.
The appeasement of the dark goddess in this way
was primarily because of her role as the sorceress
of the afterlife, but true believers also feared
Hecate's ability to afflict the mind with madness
(as in the Dionystic curses), as well as her influence over the night creatures. That is to say, offerings were made to Hecate because she was
thought to govern haunted places where evil or
murderous activity occurred. Such areas where vio-
lence or lechery had a history were believed to be
magnets of malevolent spirits, something like
"haunted houses," and if one wanted to get along
with the resident apparitions they needed to make
oblations to the ruler of the darkness, Hecate.
The acceptance of the oblations was announced
by Hecate's familiar (the night owl), and the spooky
sound of the creature was perceived as a good
omen by those who gathered on the eve of the full
moon. Statues of the goddess bearing the triple-
face of a dog, a snake, and a horse, overshadowed
the dark rituals when they were performed at the
crossing of three roads. At midnight, Hecate's
devotees left food offerings at the intersection for
the goddess ("Hecate's Supper"), and, once de-
posited, quickly exited without turning around or
looking back.

Sometimes the offerings consisted of honey
cakes and chicken hearts, at other times puppies,
honey, and female black lambs were slaughtered

for the goddess and her strigae. The strigae were deformed and vicious owl-like affiliates of Hecate who flew through the night feeding on the bodies of unattended babies. During the day the strigae appeared as simple old women, and such folklore may account for the history of flying witches. The same strigae hid amidst the leaves of the trees during the annual festival of Hecate (held on August 13), when Hecate's followers offered up the highest praise of the goddess. Hecate's devotees celebrated such festivals near Lake Averna in Campania where the sacred willow groves of the goddess stood, and they communed with the tree spirits (earth spirits, including Hecate, were thought to inhabit trees) and summoned the souls of the dead from the mouths of nearby caves. It was here that Hecate was known as Hecate-Chthonia ("Hecate of the earth"), a depiction in which she most clearly embodied the popular earth-mother-spirit, which conversed through the cave-stones and sacred willow trees.

Whereas Hecate was known elsewhere as Hecate-Propylaia, "the one before the gate," a role in which she guarded the entrances of homes and temples from nefarious outside evils (talk about Satan casting out Satan!); and whereas she was also known as Hecate-Propolos, "the one who leads," as in the underworld guide of Persephone and of those who inhabit graveyards; and finally she was known as Hecate-Phosphoros, "the light bearer," her most sacred title and one which recalls another powerful underworld spirit, Satan, whose original name was Lucifer ("the light bearer"); it was nevertheless her role as the feminist earth-goddess-spirit Hecate-Chthonia that popularized her divinity and commanded such reverence from common people.

Such popular religious concepts of earth-spirits inhabiting trees, soliciting incantation and ritual, and revealing abstruse secrets, is an idea familiar to students of eastern mythology. The following chapter will discuss the revival of such paganistic notions, and, more importantly, will attempt to answer the disturbing question: Do the ancient spirits of the gods and goddesses converse with modern man?

Important Notes Regarding the Gods of Greece

The following notes on the Greek deities are important and relate to the remaining chapters of the book.

From the example of Gaia we learn: 1) Gaia was the original Greek "mother earth"; 2) she was worshipped as a literal spirit; 3) her body (the planet earth) was made to contain the elder spirits of the Titans; and 4) such spirits were known to communicate through trees, streams (etc.), and various idols.

From the example of Zeus we learn: 1) Zeus, among other things, was the king or "prince of the air" and the "god of thunder," titles biblically and historically associated with Satan; 2) his altar at Pergamum may have been the "throne of Satan" mentioned in Revelation 2:13; 3) he was an oracle spirit and communicated through trees, streams, and other nature devices; and 4) he was ritually associated with transsexualism through his lover Leto.

From the example of Apollo we learn: 1) Apollo

was the most important oracle god in Greece; 2) his oracle at Delphi was the most famous in antiquity; 3) his pythian prophetesses popularized the social status of mediums (psychics); 4) natural hallucinogens used as instruments of paranormal communication was a part of his spirituality; 5) his gospel was humanistic: "know yourself," "do nothing in excess," and "don't get in a hurry," were the basic rules; 6) unlike the Hebrew prophets, the Delphic "psychics" commercialized the prophetic gifts and charged for their services; and 7) Apollo's son, Asclepius, combined earth elements, spirit-guide animals (especially serpents), energy channeling, incantation, and psychic dreams, with healing.

From the example of Dionysus we learn: 1) the uses of wine, sensuality, song, and revelry, were combined with having a "religious experience"; 2) Dionysus' feminist devotees, the Bacchae, challenged the traditional roles of women by dressing transvestite, behaving violently masculine, and disregarding virtuous sexuality; 3) the Bacchae embraced physical pleasures including the drink, the dance, the song, and lesbianism, at the expense of their children; 4) the Bacchae practiced magic, embraced evil, destroyed children, and profaned the sacred, in the name of women's rights; and 5) they manipulated others (magically imprisoned their souls) for personal gain.

From the example of Demeter we learn: 1) Demeter was the popular goddess of the environment; 2) her rituals and rewards taught people to tune in with, and care for, the planet; 3) her doctrines involved an amalgam of human energy, superstition, and mystical earth forces; 4) she, along with Gaia, Hera, Artemis, Hecate, and others, incarnated the earth's fertility forces within the goddess images; 5) the Bible reveals that such forces are demonic and seek communion with mankind; and 6) this was illustrated in the myths, behaviors, and rituals of the goddesses, especially of Hecate.

Notes

1. Richard Cavendish, *Man, Myth & Magic*, s.v. "Zeus."

2. Ibid., [The same page as preceding note.]

3. Ibid., s.v. "Zeus."

4. Thomas R. Horn, *Spiritual Warfare—The Invisible Invasion* (Lafayette, LA: Huntington House Publishers, 1998), 23-24.

5. Richard Cavendish, *Man, Myth & Magic*, s.v. "Apollo."

6. Euripides, *The Bacchantes*, Dramatis Personare (Messenger to Pentheus concerning the Bacchantes), B.C. 410.

7. Walter F. Otto, *Dionysus Myth and Cult* (Indianapolis, IN: Indiana University Press, 1965), 114.

8. Ibid., 169.

9. Ibid., 116.

10. Lucius Apuleius, *The Golden Asse*, Book Eleven, 1566.

11. *The Hymns of Homer, XXX*, Chapter 11: 1-19.

12. Apollonius Rhodius, *Argonautica*, translated by R.C. Seaton (Cambridge MA: Harvard University Press, 1912), 1026-1062; 1191-1224.

The Old Gods of the New Age

"The kind of events that once took place will by reason of human nature take place again."
—Thucydides

A few years ago during the Christmas season, my wife, Nita, and I, walked through a local mall. As we perused the different shops, we came across a New Age bookstore conducting a "Grand Opening." In a derisive tone, I said to my wife, "Can you believe the lack of intelligence of some people?" I strolled casually into the store, and without hesitation, snatched a book from the shelf and began offering a sarcastic commentary as I read from the pages. When I noticed that Nita was growing uncomfortable, I placed the book back on the shelf and proceeded out of the store. Suddenly, a dull sensation hit me. It began in my stomach and shot upward through my cranium, impacting my equilibrium. As I stepped outside onto the main mall walkway, my head started to spin, my hands began to shake, and I felt as if I were going to faint. It was literally as if an invisible terror had "jumped" on me, and was somehow injecting powerful feelings of nausea and anxiety throughout my entire body. I tried to shake it off, but couldn't. I attempted to walk it off, and failed. At last, feigning interest in something, I moved away from my wife and began to pray. I asked the Lord to forgive me for my sarcastic attitude, for my lack of caution, and for my want of concern for the lost. I prayed for deliverance from evil and for a healing of the body and mind. After several hours of such walking and praying, I was finally restored. I discovered a valuable lesson that day: while it's true that a Christian cannot be demon-possessed, it's equally true that the "princes" of this world are powerful, and we should enter their arena only after prayer, and at the prompting of the Lord. I also learned the mystical forces of the New Age movement are genuine (and willing to protect their territory!), and that much of what is currently published under the guise of New Age "enlightenment," is nothing less than Old Age doctrines of nefarious, invisible hosts.

As in antiquity, so in modern times, those who practice paganism are guilty of worshipping "devils" (Rev. 9:20). The dogma, which were once embraced (and still are, through the New Age Movement) as the wisdom of the gods, are defined in the scriptures as the "doctrines of devils." The Apostle Paul declared: "The things which the Gentiles sacrifice, they sacrifice to devils" (1 Cor. 10:20). In Acts 7:41-42 (Jerusalem Bible), we find that those who worship idols are joined to the "army of heaven" [stratos, the "fallen angel army"], and Psalm 96:5 concludes that "all the gods of the nations are idols" (elilim, LXX daimonia [demons]). Thus, pagan images, such as represented the ancient gods and goddesses, were

elilim (empty, nothing, vanity), but behind the
empty idols were the living dynamics of idolatry,
and spiritual objects of heathen adoration, the
daimonia (demons) of the Bible.

Since the Bible clearly defines idolatry as the
worship of demons, and since demons are eternal
personalities that desire the worship of men, it is
fair to conclude the characterization of such deities as "Zeus," "Amun-Ra," "Demeter," and "Isis,"
were simply the classical names attributed to specific fallen spirits. In other words, Apollo was a
real personality; Osiris was a genuine underworld
fiend; Hecate actually lived, and still does! One
also concludes that the images of the gods (falcon-
headed statues, animal forms, etc.) served the
purposes of such spirits by providing a point of
focus, and by revealing the "nature" of the particular spirit existing within the god. The iconog-
raphies, myths, and rituals of each deity exhibited
the specific characteristics (nature, gender, underworld authority, etc.) of that particular entity. Thus,
the myths and images of Zeus, according to such
theory, were the physical manifestations of a literal demon of air, while statues of the goddess
Demeter represented an earth spirit. It is my as-
sertion, and the claim of this book, that the same
spirits of antiquity, including Zeus, Athene,
Dionysus, and others, continue to express themselves within modern paganism. Dr. Jones agrees,
asserting that the connection between the New
Age Movement and the gods of mythology is
strong. "Nothing has changed in Satan's game
plan," says Jones, "just the names of the players,
and, in some instances, even the names are the
same."

Paganism in America is exploding as we approach the new millennium. Throughout Hollywood, government, cyberspace, and even the church, people rush to embrace the religious philosophies of the New Age of Aquarius. As a modernistic process by which the old gods are worshipped, the New Age Movement emerged in the United States during the 1960s, and has experienced a steady growth ever since. The broad appeal of the New Age Movement as a Western phenomenon can be explained to some degree as the result of a changing culture. Americans have gradually abandoned the fundamental precepts of Christianity (prayer in school, Bible in courts, etc.), which provided the cornerstone of civil life and jurisprudence in American society for more than 200 years. As a generation of baby-boomers has focused on human potential and the "god within us all," Eastern philosophies of Monism, Pantheism, Hinduism, and self-realization, continue to provide Americans, and even some Christians, with an alluring opportunity to throw off the "outdated ideas" of fundamental Christianity and to espouse a more "enlightened" world view of God and reality.

Some of the most notable celebrities have joined the political ambitions of the New Age Movement (goals include a United Nation's sponsored Environmental Sabbath for the Goddess Earth), including Shirly MacLaine, Dick Gregory, Lindsay Wagner, Dennis Weaver, Dirk Benedict, Cloris Leachman, Richard Gere, Ally Sheedy, and the late John Denver. Many mainstream "Christian" denominations have also annexed the New Age ideas, and believers who once held strong doctrinal positions of the supremacy of Christ, have abandoned those views in exchange for a New Age universal philosophy.

Examples include a witch who teaches principles of goddess worship at a Roman Catholic college in California, and United Methodist pastors who propose replacing the name of Jesus with Sophia (Goddess of Wisdom) when reading about the crucifixion. Such persons claim we should join the efforts of New Agers and be sympathetic to "Goddess-minded Christians." Former New Age devotee, Judy Vorfeld re-discovered the real Jesus after embracing such ideas. She became involved in freelance writing as a result of experiencing the dangers involved in participating in the New Age Movement. For many years she actively avoided anything to do with the Christianity of her childhood. When she was in her early forties, a neighborhood minister said he was starting a new church, and she thought the time might be right to look at Christianity again. Judy writes:

> For a time I was involved in a fellowship that worshipped a different deity than the God of the Bible. . . . I joined a church that evolved from ecumenism to religious syncretism. . . . Six months after I became part of the fellowship, fundamental Christianity was retired in favor of a universal religious system, one designed to be inoffensive to people of any theological persuasion. The fellowship then put together a creed that would be acceptable for any visitors coming to worship with us. Jews, Hindus, Muslims, and Buddhists were welcome, as were Theosophists, Rosicrucians,

and Hare Krishnas. ... Our minister
brought a popular seminar, advertised a
self-improvement course into our church.
Most of us were impressed with the profes-
sional manner of the leaders and their
sophisticated system of teaching self-
realization. ... The organization's format,
we were told, held the answers to all our
problems. ... Church leadership eagerly
blended the organization's ideas into an
agenda that became a part of our church
curriculum. Eastern meditation, Psychic
healing, and guided imagery were all practiced.[1]

Judy Vorfeld is a friend of mine and has provided me with guidance on the New Age Movement. In recent correspondence, she described
modern Druids, and spoke of their methods of
magic healing through "visualization." She con-
fessed:

Tom. ... When we were involved in Silva
Mind Control [through her local church],
we did the same thing [visualized healing].
At that time, I thought God was behind all
this stuff. I 'saw' people in my mind's eye
who had various diseases, and I sent energy to heal them. In groups like this, the
leader often has a list of people who are
sick. This gives them a way to follow
through and see who was healed. I have no
doubt some people were healed, but since
we were invoking a power other than that
of the real God, what were we doing?"

What indeed?

An amazing component of the New Age Movement (as verified by such examples as my friend, Judy's) is its capacity to adapt to a variety of religious, even Christian, ideas. Consequently, many of the popular "Christian" doctrines advocated today are nothing more than the cultic propositions of Eastern mysticism and ancient paganism. These include concepts of psychic healing, self-realization, emotional experiences, rules of success, breathing techniques, positive confession, name it and claim it, environmental theology, the ecumenical movement, visualization, hypnosis by clergy, mind manipulation, and so on. At times, and I say this with caution, even the activity within the "fundamental" church, including certain physical phenomena we sometimes embrace as the miraculous evidence of "revival," is a modern form of magic and opens the door for "old gods" and their mysticism to invade the church. The line between a true manifestation of God, and human orchestration, is often blurred. Sincere people, in a quest to experience God, frequently mimic the doctrinal and physical activity of others. Some physical phenomena (crawling on the church floor and making animal sounds, etc.) is extra-biblical in nature (not everything that is extra-biblical is un-biblical, however) and therefore undefined by New Testament teachings.

As a result, some Christians have been drawn to mystical experiences rather than concentrating on God and His Word. Even sermons preached by well-meaning ministers have tempted Christians to pursue "supernatural" encounters with God, rather than instructing them to live by faith. The danger of such undisciplined sincerity is that human nature rarely limits its opportunity for experience. If the Bible has no clear guidelines of conduct and order, and the activity is being promoted by church authorities as a way of experiencing God, then the person seeking the experience may have trouble defining what is, and what isn't acceptable, and thus go too far. For emotional people, the experience may be expressed by a physical reaction, while academics tend to interpret mystical experiences with God as divine revelations or imparted knowledge. The dangerous consequences of such conduct often leads to religious behavior more reminiscent of Dionysus or Apollo worship than of New Testament Christianity. As a result, people like Judy Vorfeld start out in a Christian church and wind up in the New Age movement.

The dangers of mysticism, such as those inherent with emphasizing experiences over doctrine, were soundly illustrated in a recent report by Samantha Smith. She writes:

> I became strongly concerned about this movement after observing a "service" at a south Denver Vineyard church.... [a woman] stood in the middle of a group of people who ran their hands over her body (within an inch or so of the clothing), then kept swooshing some invisible thing toward her heart area. Saddened, I walked toward the door, where a church member said, "You should come back on Sunday night. That's when they levitate." . . . [another group] in Seattle . . . sit in circles, clucking, flapping their tucked arms and visualizing themselves hatching the "Man Child Com-

pany," a heretical Manifested Sons of God concept. In Kansas City, a pastor watched in horror as men and women lay on the floor with their knees up and legs spread apart, trying to birth the same thing. . . . I tape-recorded a group of Episcopalians howling at the moon, like wolves, giving a "Howl-le-lu-ia Chorus" for Earth Day. It gets worse. There are reports of "holy vomiting" (seance ectoplasm?) and of Christians becoming demonized by being "slain in the spirit." How can this be?[2]

I share Samantha Smith's concerns. Recently I was approached by a young man during a Sunday morning service (at a church which stresses supernatural "experiences" as a test of one's spirituality) and was told how, he, and other members of the "intercessory prayer group," were experiencing temporary possessions (?) of evil spirits. When I asked him what he meant, he stated that evil spirits were "coming out of people, and, as they do, they are going into us [the people in the prayer room] and then speaking out loud." When I asked for clarification, he repeated that evil "spirits" were audibly conversing through him and other members of the prayer group during the Sunday morning church services! I warned him of the dangers of mysticism and reminded him that the Jews were forbidden to communicate with spirits. I strongly advised him not to allow any spirit (other than the Holy Spirit) to speak through him, and showed him how Michael the archangel did not discourse with the devil, but said, "The Lord rebuke thee" (Jude 9). I'm unsure if the young man followed my instruction, but the episode illustrates how a church environment emphasizing supernatural experiences over sound biblical doctrine can create an atmosphere conducive to New Age mysticism, mediumism, spiritism, and paganism. I believe the young man was earnest, and it's my understanding that the "medium" practices at the church have ended.

Gaia, Hathor, and Demeter Live!
New Age Earth Worship

The majority of New Age mysticism and other forms of modern paganism (the ongoing worship of the gods and goddesses) is unquestionably occurring outside of the fundamentalist church. Expressions of neo-paganism ranging from self-help organizations working with large corporations to offer stress management symposiums to their employees using the principles of the New Age Movement to produce positive harmony, prosperity, and overall business success, to other not-so-subtle forms of paganism, such as those practiced by WICCA and the Women's Spirituality Movement, account for more than 600,000 women nationwide participating in the invocation of ancient earth-goddesses, including Demeter, Aphrodite, and Isis.

Retail stores springing up in faddish malls across the United States supply replica idols of the popular female deities, and marketing of the occultic paraphernalia used in venerating the goddesses (crystals, candles, books of spells, etc.) has become a multimillion dollar industry. Dimly lit "occult" bookstores that once inhabited shabby old buildings have been replaced with trendy New Age shops located amidst the most fashionable strip malls in the nicest areas of town. One such store, Necromance, is located at stylish Melrose Avenue in Los Angeles, and business is booming with sales of "human fingers on a leather cord, necklaces of human teeth, bone beads, human skulls and even a tiny fetal one."[3] The Necromance, and similar New Age businesses, are attentively supported by a growing population of neo-pagans and teachers of the arcane rites. Store owners are generally New Agers or practicing witches, and many have been publicly embraced by politicians, religious leaders, and Hollywood entertainers. Not long ago, one such witch claimed to be a temple prostitute of the goddess Astarte and performed sequential ritual earth-magic sex with 251 men at the University of Southern California.

In her book, *Goddess Earth*, Samantha Smith connected the pagan agenda of the Earth Summit, the Environmental Movement, and the current mix of politics and public education, with the New Age Movement's goals of a revival of Mother Earth worship under a united World Order. After attending a lecture by Miriam Starhawk (a teacher of the "ancient craft") at the University of Denver, she wrote:

> Miriam Starhawk, who calls herself "a goddess-worshipping pagan witch," appeared at the University of Denver to lecture. . . . about her concerns on "Magic, Sex and Politics." . . . There was a time, she said, thousands of years ago, when people lived in harmony with the earth and each other. They practiced magic and used the art of evoking power from within, trancing, and became one with the balance of things.

When they turned from the goddess, all
havoc broke loose. Men ruled over women
and other men. They waged endless wars.
People splintered into rich and poor, free
and slave, powerful and powerless. The
witchess (goddesses) were battered, raped,
tortured, burned, poisoned, and dismem-
bered. And so, the Earth herself nearly died.
But, she was not destroyed! Some continued to practice [earth-centered magic] in
secret. . . . [and now] Just at a time when
the final destruction of the earth is prob-
able and nearly inevitable, women are re-
membering the goddess [Mother Earth].
They are crying out against the war and
the destruction of the human race. "The
reborn are walking the Earth in new forms
and the witches arise and dance (skyclad)
in the open. The Goddess has not come to
save us. It is up to us to save Her [the
earth]."[4]

Today, New Agers ask, "If God is our Father,
then who is our Mother?", and they happily answer, "Earth!" Not surprisingly, the worship of the
earth's "spirit" as a nurturing goddess mother has
been revived as a central feature of paganism.
Earth Day 1990, celebrated the start of the decade
by coordinating nearly 200 million people world-
wide into a universal effort aimed at saving "our
endangered Mother Earth." Christian leaders
signed "Green Pledges," and Wiccan witches performed arcane rituals in honor of the Earth Goddess, Gaia. Interest in such contraptions as the
sweat lodge, a device used by several ancient religions, including many American Indian tribes,
as an apparatus whereby one re-enters the womb

Athene, by Brooke Townsend

of the Earth Mother, was celebrated. Such famous
personalities as Ted Turner and Jane Fonda built
their own private sweat lodges, and were praised
for following the primitive and simple pattern of
furrowing a womblike "nest" into the surface of
the earth and covering it with a dome of natural
materials. The entry into Ms. Fonda's lodge was
intentionally kept so low as to simulate the birthing
experience during exit, and the ground inside
was left uncovered so as to allow the inhabitants
the opportunity of getting in touch with the all-
knowing Earth Spirit.

The sweat lodge method of communing with
the sacred Earth Mother, Gaia, as practiced by
various ancient religions and New Age devotees,
includes sitting in a semi-circle around heated
stones inside the lodge, and entering into a mystical state of consciousness. As with ancient
pythians, the prophetesses of Apollo, the altered
mental condition is accomplished through repeti-
tive chanting, drumming, and breathing the fumes
of natural stimulants, such as peyote. Spirit animals, called "power animals" by New Agers and
American Indians, are called upon to guide the
soul through the underworld journey, or "vision
quest," and participants are encouraged to "dance
their animal" for revelations and healing of the
body and mind. Such animal dancing is accomplished by allowing the spirit of the creature to
enter into, and take control of, the participant.

Dr. Leslie Gray, a noted University instructor
and female shaman (something like a witch doc-
tor), employs such uses of "animal dancing" in the
psychiatric (shamanic) treatment of her patients.
She described the positive results of animal danc-

ing in the case of one insecure young woman, saying, "I lay down on the ground next to her and put us both into an altered state of consciousness via a tape of drumming. I came back from my 'journey' and blew the spirit of a mountain lion into [her]. I then instructed her to go out into nature and dance her animal. . . . [and when she did] She no longer felt afraid of people."[5]

Such uses of animal images and other natural products in the worship of the Great Earth Mother is by design. New Age pagans, drawing on Eastern philosophies and the occult, believe that, unlike the evil human race, such elements are at one with Gaia. According to them, if it were not for the male-dominated, styrofoam- producing, beef-eating, gas-guzzling, bulldozer-driving destroyers of the rainforests (human beings), the earth would be a better place. Natural earth-centered resources, such as animals, crystals, and even colors, are thus the products of choice for the students of New Age earth-magic. For instance, light blue is the color of Mother Earth's sky, thus Wiccans burn candles of light blue to acquire her magic tranquility or understanding. Red candles are burned for strength or sexual love, and green candles for financial assistance, etc. Instruments of magic, such as magic wands, are also made of Mother Earth's natural supply, usually of Willow, Oak, or fruit tree branches. Magic potions employed during the witches' Esbats (earth-celebrations held during the new and full moons) also contain the Earth's natural byproducts, including clover, olive oil, grape juice, garlic cloves, and rosebuds. Finally, special ceremonies conducted at the crossing of three earth-paths (remember the triple-path earth-

Diana, by Brooke Townsend

mother, Hecate?) are dedicated to the Mother Earth goddesses, Gaia, Demeter, Persephone, Isis, Aphrodite, Hathor, Hera, Diana, Athene, and Hecate. While such rituals are gender-inclusive, they are specifically designed to elevate the goddess, or female spirit. In fact, an enlightening component of nearly every form of goddess-earth worship is the absence of male leadership. Goddess deities, especially the ones that exhibit independence of the male presence, are cheerfully exalted during the worship of Gaia. Athene, the manly goddess of Olympus, and Diana (Artemis), the lesbian[6] earth-goddess and patroness of witches, are considered especially important during the contemporary worship of the Earth Goddess. Venerating such "she-devils" is more widespread than ever, and anyone visiting the local university library, the area bookstore, the internet, or Saturday morning cartoons, will undoubtedly discover the presence and deification of Mother Earth. The effect of New Age cartoons on young people is particularly disturbing, as it teaches innocent kids the principles of paganism. Characters such as Captain Planet and the Planeteers tell children to use their "mystical powers" to protect the environment, and to assist Gaia, the motherly earth-spirit, in her quest to join forces with Captain Planet and his "special children" to save the earth from middle-aged capitalist swine (there go those rotten adults again!) who want to destroy the loving Mother Earth. Each episode of Captain Planet ends by encouraging kids to help Gaia and the Planeteers save the earth from evildoers. The new animated Superman, that once proud defender of "truth, justice, and the American way," has also seen the light, and, evidently, converted to New Age mysticism. His girlfriend, Lois Lane, consults the "white Wiccan coven" for information or magic to assist in Superman's task.

The Burning Man

For the past ten years such earth-worshipping pagans, and their little cartoon-watching pagans, have migrated from Canada, Brazil, Germany, Russia, and 25 other countries, to an isolated corner of Black Rock Desert in Nevada, where a four-day-long New Age techno-fest known as "The Burning Man" has been conducted. Attendance at the 1997 pagan carnival included an estimated 15,000 Wiccans, Satanists, Goddesses (white witches), nudists, and a consortium of other lost party-goers, who converge on the hot Nevada desert for a Labor Day weekend of "glorious Hell on earth." The number of participants at the Burning Man gala has nearly doubled each year since 1986, and, by the year 2000, organizers hope to break 30,000. The Burning Man is a no-holds-barred New Age "Woodstock" style festival, where neo-pagans, Wiccans, transvestite entertainers, back-slidden Christians, and a host of homosexuals, go to trance, perform rituals, burn sacrifices to idols, dance in the nude, engage in sex, and otherwise "express" themselves and become one with Gaia.

Attendees set up theme camps such as "Lost Vegas," "Motel 666," and "Crucifixion with a Celebrity" (where one can purchase a picture of a crucified obese Elvis). Hamburgers are sold by devil-worshipping pagans at the McSatan cafe, and T-shirts are available that proudly proclaim, "Praise the Whore." The Burning Man itself is a forty-foot-high effigy of the "Spirit Cave Man" (sacred to local Indians and New Agers) which is torched, together with just about everything else, at the close of the festivities.

George Otis Jr., president of The Sentinel Group (a Christian research agency), attended the 1996 Burning Man festival with a colleague. He wrote of the experience:

> On Saturday night, the hell-themed 1996 festival reached its crescendo in the form of a drama. . . . These people were literally celebrating the fact that one day they would enter hell. To simulate their journey, the camp's center stage was transformed into the "Vestibule of Hell." The guest of honor was none other than "Papa Satan." . . . As the lecherous Papa Satan bowed in mock chains before a placard reading "Believe in the Lord Jesus Christ and thou shalt be saved," a group called "Idiot Flesh," [supposedly Christians] dressed as hooded executioners, began to play a discordant dirge accompanied by flashing strobes. When the crowd started its torchlight procession toward the Gates of Hell and an eerie, sculpted castle called The City of Dis, I sensed an unmistakable chill in the air. Our march had been joined by unseen, malevolent guests. . . . nudist and a moving sea of devil banners [also] moved around us. . . . At the tri-tower City of Dis, our descent into the Inferno reached a demonic sanctuary. . . . While massive loudspeakers pumped out a hellish bass tone accompanied by tormented screams . . . people dressed as de-

monic insects celebrated by copulating with other captured souls. It was a scene that looked as if it had been plucked from a horrific nightmare. Mesmerized by the evocative music, the performers began to chant, "Devil's delight, fire tonight!" Wood piles inside the towers of Dis were ignited, causing orange flames to belch forth from the eyes and mouths of demonic gargoyles built onto the turrets. As the heat became more intense, the entourage danced around the towers. Satan had defeated the church.[7]

Otis continued the report by confessing, "I had to remind myself that what I had witnessed at the Burning Man Festival was happening right here in the United States, not in the temples of India or the deserts of Sinai." He also admits that he met many friendly, creative, and intelligent people at the Burning Man festival, and he encourages believers to contend for such lost souls in prayer.

Zeus, Osiris, and Apollo Live!
New Age Oracles

"What advantage then hath the Jew? . . . Much every way: chiefly, because that unto them were committed the oracles of God" (Rom. 3:1-2). When the apostle Paul wrote to the church at Rome concerning the oracles (*logion*, "divine utterances") that God gave to the Jews, he was referring to the revelations of the Old Testament Law and Prophets. In the Bible, the word "oracle" means supernatural utterance. It can also refer to a device used in the production of divine utterances. The Bible is an oracle, as was the Urim and Thummim (sacred devices) of the Old Testament. When a man or a woman speaks as true prophets of God, he or she is likewise considered "an oracle of God" (1 Peter 4:11).

New Age pagans, such as those who attend the Burning Man Festival, are extremely interested in such oracular phenomena, and readily accept certain portions of the Bible as divinely oracular (the verses they believe support their ideas of God, reincarnation, spirit communing, and the afterlife). But, in the quest for spiritual knowledge, modern pagans also reach out beyond the "confines" of the Bible into a veiled world of mystical utterances, table-tapping, ouija boards, psychic phone lines, visualization, channeling, and other esoteric forms of prognostication.

I once preached a sermon on oracles and the "death of the Olympian gods." I boldly proclaimed that Christianity had swept the globe, and that, as far as I knew, not a living person remained on earth that bowed in reverence to Apollo, or consulted at his sacred shrines. The sermon was received with rousing applause by the audience, and I sold some tapes. The only problem was, I was wrong. Apollo's Oracle at Delphi, the most famous oracle of antiquity, is in ruins. But the worship of the Olympian god, and the order of his pythian priestesses, are actively involved in Wiccan and New Age paganism in the 1990s. The fact is, it's unclear if the worship of Apollo or the consulting of his oracles ever ceased.

There is some evidence that generational witches may have continued the worship of Apollo and the secrets of his pythian divination for centuries. Whether or not that's true, the admirers of

Apollo number in the tens of thousands today.
This is primarily because Apollo is an oracle god,
and his disciples are granted a "divine audience."
Unlike other underworld spirits, Apollo audibly
communicates (at times with amazing accuracy in
antiquity) through the vocal chords of the pythoness to his followers. This characteristic originally
caused, and apparently continues to cause, a tremendous cult popularity for Apollo. The Greek
historian, Herodotus (considered the father of
history), wrote of an interesting event. Croesus,
the king of Lydia, expressed doubt regarding the
accuracy of Apollo's Oracle at Delphi. To test the
oracle, Croesus sent messengers to inquire of the
pythian prophetess as to what he, the king, was
doing on a certain day. The priestess surprised
the king's messengers by visualizing the question,
and by formulating the answer, before they arrived. A portion of the historian's account reads:

> The moment that the Lydians (the mes-
> sengers of Croesus) entered the sanctuary,
> and before they put their questions, the
> Pythoness thus answered them in hexam-
> eter verse: ". . . Lo! on my sense there
> striketh the smell of a shell- covered tor-
> toise, Boiling now on a fire, with the flesh
> of a lamb, in a cauldron. Brass is the vessel
> below, and brass the cover above it." These
> words the Lydians wrote down at the mouth
> of the Pythoness as she prophesied, and then
> set off on their return to Sardis. . . . [when]
> Croesus undid the rolls. . . . [he] instantly
> made an act of adoration . . . declaring that
> the Delphic was the only really oracular
> shrine. . . . For on the departure of his mes-
> sengers he had set himself to think what

was most impossible for any one to conceive of his doing, and then, waiting till the
day agreed on came, he acted as he had
determined. He took a tortoise and a lamb,
and cutting them in pieces with his own
hands, boiled them together in a brazen
cauldron, covered over with a lid which
was also of brass. (Herodotus, book 1: 47)

The demon Apollo established an enormous
following through such prophetic trickery, and,
evidently, continues to do so. On the Internet,
there are numerous Web sites dedicated to the
modern worship of Apollo, and some such sites
teach the methods and sacred locations of current
pythian oracular activity.

Modern pagans are drawn to oracles because
oracles ostensibly prove the existence of a spirit
world, and because they seemingly provide a
method of communicating with such spirits.
Besides the pythian, ancient oracles being revived
by the participants of New Age paganism include
interpreting the flame of candles, the organs of
animals, the behavior of water, and the wisping of
wind through the leaves of trees. Tree oracles,
such as the necromantic oak tree of Zeus at
Dodona, were among the most popular oracles of
the ancient world. This was due in part to the
belief that the root of the tree extended into the
lower world, and the tree was thus connected to
the underworld dead. Judy Vorfeld admitted
communing with tree spirits when she was involved
in New Age mysticism. As a biblical endorsement
of the activity, New Agers erroneously claim that
2 Samuel 5:24 is a scriptural account of King David
consulting with tree oracles, and they point out

that Jehovah instructed David to "smite the host
of the Philistines" after he heard "the sound of a
going in the tops of the mulberry trees."

Angels are another popular oracular entity of
New Agers. Literally dozens of New Age books
describe methods of communicating with the spirit
world through the "assistance" of angels. Such
book titles are self explanatory: *Ask Your Angels: A
Practical Guide to Working with the Messengers of
Heaven to Empower and Enrich Your Life,* and, *The
Angels Within Us: A Spiritual Guide to the Twenty-two
Angels that Govern Our Lives.* In one publication,
we discover the interesting "identity" of such
governing spirits as the author describes an
encounter with his angel-oracle:

> The swirling fog began to dissipate, and I
> could see the flicker of a light ahead—a
> darting, pulsating glow resembling a fire-
> fly. I paused for a moment to observe, and
> the tiny flare expanded in size and ap-
> peared as a small full moon touching the
> earth. As I moved closer to the radiance, it
> suddenly changed into a vertical beam, a
> pillar of transparent light.
>
> "Are you the angel I am seeking?" I asked.
> The soft yet powerful feminine voice re-
> plied,
>
> "I am the Angel of Creative Wisdom."
>
> "Do you have a name?
>
> "Some have called me Isis," she said, and
> with those words the pillar of light slowly
> materialized to reveal the face and form of
> a beautiful woman wearing a flowing white
> robe trimmed in gold.[8]

Can you believe it? "Isis" is identified as a New Age angel! Satan is clever. While such angel-oracles are undoubtedly popular among New Age devotees, the most curious form of oracular activity reinvigorated by pagans today is the "psychomanteum;" a simple, yet eerie, idea. A chair, placed in front of a large mirror in a dark room, serves as the oracle. Once positioned on the chair, the occupant stares into the mirror and waits for contact with the ghosts of the departed. In ancient times, the psychomanteum's mirror-system of communicating with "spirits" was employed by primitive Greeks in gloomy underground caverns called "halls of visions." Standing in front of a shining metal surface or caldron, grieving ancients saw and spoke with familiar apparitions.

The Sumerians, Egyptians, and Romans employed similar oracles of polished crystal, brass mirrors, and pools of water. Some argue that the Apostle Paul was referring to such mirror-oracles when he said, "For now we see through a glass, darkly; but then face to face: now I know in part; but then shall I know even as also I am known" (1 Cor. 13:12). The New Age psychomanteum is likewise used to facilitate contact with deceased relatives or family members and is increasingly being encouraged by New Age psychiatrists as a method for dealing with grief. Sometimes, under nefarious conditions, the mirror-contact phenomenon spontaneously occurs. As a teenager, my wife was involved in a horrific accident that killed her dad and sister. Following the accident, her eleven-year-old sister "materialized" in the bedroom mirror on two occasions. Since the house she lived in was

formerly occupied by gypsies, my wife believes
this fact contributed to the spontaneous
psychomanteum activity.

In his book, *Reunions,* Raymond Moody pro-
motes the use of the New Age psychomanteum as
an oracle. He has documented the experiences of
more than three hundred users of the device, and
points out that 50 percent claim to have been
contacted by a deceased relative or friend during
the first try. People interviewed by Moody include
physicians, teachers, housewives, business owners,
and law enforcement officials. One such witness,
an accountant who grieved over his departed
mother a year after her death, testified of his
experience with the psychomanteum:

> There is no doubt that the person I saw in
> the mirror was my mother! I don't know
> where she came from, but I am convinced
> that what I saw was the real person. She
> was looking out at me from the mirror. . . . I
> could tell she was in her late 70s, about the
> same age as. . . . when she died. However,
> she looked happier and healthier than she
> had at the end of her life. Her lips didn't
> move, but she spoke to me and I clearly
> heard what she had to say. She said, "I am
> fine," and smiled. . . . I stayed as relaxed as
> I could and just looked at her. . . . Then I
> decided to talk to her. I said, "It's good to
> see you again."
>
> "It s good to see you, too," she replied.
> That was it. She simply disappeared.[9]

A physician was unexpectedly contacted by a
nephew while seated in a psychomanteum:

> I suddenly had a very strong sense of the presence of my nephew, who had committed suicide. . . . I heard his voice very clearly. He greeted me and brought me a very simple message. He said, "Let my mother know that I am fine and that I love her very much." This experience was profound. I know he was there with me.[10]

Although the Bible warns of communicating with "familiar spirits" and of consulting mediums, the revival of ancient oracles, and the experiences being drawn from them, are especially seductive curiosities to the followers of New Age paganism. Communications with the dead, channeling, trancing, near-death experiences, and other forms of mediumship, harmonize a coveted and reassuring New Age theme, "I'm fine now," "All is well," "I'm waiting for you." New Agers and neo-pagans cherish such next-life universalism, and, while they typically reject the Judeo-Christian Hell, they willingly embrace the message of the oracle gods, Osiris, Zeus, and Apollo, which tell them that everyone eventually goes to "heaven."

Dionysus, Asclepius, and Hecate Live! New Age Mysticism

A spirit of mysticism has been present in the United States for generations. Like an insidious cancer, unseen, patient, deadly, it has grown. Indications of its presence have been felt occasionally, and confirmations of its actuality have been documented from Washington D.C. to Portland, Oregon. By tracing city-name origins, such as Ceres, Alexandria, Mars, Fortuna, and Media, one discovers the early influence of such mysticism within the United States. By looking at sites such as the House of the Temple, the home office of Scottish Rite Freemasonry, one discovers a continuation of the ancient occultism. Located several blocks from the White House on 16th Street in Washington D.C., the House of the Temple contains eight candelabrum fashioned after Hermes, the "god of light," as well as various other artworks reminiscent of the Temple of Dionysus. Statues of the goddesses, Isis and Nephthys, stand hallowed inside.

One can exit the House of the Temple, walk down the street and around the corner, and take pictures of an enormous obelisk (phallic Egyptian symbol of fertility) known as the Washington Monument. From there one can travel across country to Portland, Oregon, where a huge statue ("Portlandia") representing of the goddess Hecate, stands overshadowing the entrance to the City of Portland Office buildings. On the Portland City Seal, "Lady Commerce" holds a trident under a six-pointed star. Both are important instruments of Hecatian witchcraft.

To the South, in California, Athene (Minerva), the manly goddess of war, greets humans from a prominent position on the Great Seal of the State of California. Other states boasting similar Great Seals and goddesses include New York (Liberty and Justice); Oklahoma (Themis); New Jersey (Ceres and Liberty); and Florida. Even the Great Seal of the United States depicts an array of equally abstruse symbols, including an unfinished Egyptian pyramid overshadowed by the "All-Seeing Eye" and bearing the cryptic phrase, *NOVUS ORDO SECLORUM,* "A new order of the ages."

As we approach the culmination of the "new order of the ages," cult experts forecast a staggering revival of idolatry and Eastern mysticism. As church attendance declines across the United States, Buddhists, Muslims, Hindus, Theosophists, Christian Scientists, and New Agers, expand to meet the desires and mystical interests of Americans. Tarot card reading is at an all-time high. Psychic phone lines are jammed with over $300 million in calls per year, and celebrities such as LaToya Jackson and Dionne Warwick lend credibility to psychic consultations. Even the US Government has shown interest in such phenomena. During the 1995 budget cuts, the CIA was forced to release a $20 million project ("Operation Stargate") aimed at studying the usefulness of psychics in gathering military secrets from foreign powers.

The wives of two U.S. Presidents, Nancy Reagan and Hillary Clinton, have also been the subject of public examination since it was discovered that they consulted with astrologers and psychics. Hillary Clinton went so far as to channel "conversations" with the spirit of Eleanor Roosevelt. Whether such conversations included a White House psychomanteum, or other oracular device, is unknown, but the obvious widespread interest in such paranormal activity substantiates what Judy Vorfeld has said: "Dabbling in the realm of the occult is currently stylish. Even some Christians seem unable to avoid the attraction of this colorful, seductive world."[11]

The colorful seduction of mysticism is reaching into every fiber of our culture. From public school Environmental Education to faddish television good-guys, today's generation is bombarded with a New Age Occultianity (Western Christian beliefs mixed with occultism) that popularize the supernatural. Beloved comic book heroes such as "Spawn" teach our youth the dangerous Persephonian idea that a person can be in league with the devil, and still be a good person. Such doctrines of "harmonizing duality" are extremely popular (comics of "Spawn" have sold over 100 million copies) and blend nicely with the syncretistic goals of the New Age Movement. Judy Vorfeld continues:

> The mystical, make-believe world of yesteryear, whose delightful stories tickled the imaginations of generations of young people, has evolved into a magical world of pseudo-reality for people of all ages. It's seen as a world of "good" creatures having supernatural powers and using them to stamp out "evil" beings. These popular characters are displayed on such items as cereal boxes, T-shirts, glassware, jewelry, bumper stickers, bedding, school folders, and toothbrushes. . . . Television paved the way by giving us sympathetic, clever characters like Samantha, Tabitha, Endora, and Jeannie. . . . Now our culture is surrounded with supernatural cuddly toys, adorable magic elves, pastel-colored unicorns, and extraterrestrial entities who roam earth's atmosphere offering love, justice, comfort, reincarnation, and other types of eternal life.[12]

Christians must realize that powerful and ancient entities are behind such mystical playthings.

In the air above and the earth beneath are nefarious progenitors of Old/New Age mysticism. "Gods" to some and "demons" to others, such forces have numerous titles. They can appear in hideous forms or as beautiful angels of light. They are the "wicked spirits" (*poneria:* the collective body of demon soldiers comprising Satan's hordes), "rulers of darkness" (*kosmokrators:* governing spirits of darkness), "powers" (*exousia:* high ranking powers of evil), and "principalities" (*arche:* commanding generals over Satan's fallen army) of Ephesians 6:12. As the gods who walk among us, they live today and encourage mysticism among pagans, witches, New Agers, church-goers, and the general public, in at least the following ways:

Aphrodite—sensuality, fertility rites, wiccan rituals, sacred prostitution;

Amun-Ra—masturbation, self realization, environmentalism, Darwinism;

Apis—animal worship, animal rights, animal channeling, occultianity;

Apollo—humanism, oracles, channeling, psychics, drugs, visualization;

Artemis—goddess worship, animal worship, animal rights, lesbianism;

Asclepius—holistic medicine, psychic dreaming, spirit-guide animals;

Athene—goddess worship, feminism, the spirituality movement, lesbianism;

Baal—oracles, polytheism, abortion, fertility issues;

Demeter—environmental education, earth worship, goddess worship;

Dionysus—excessive wine, Freudianism, ecstasy, pornography, lesbianism, abortion;

Eros—eroticism, mystical sex, body worship, body piercing, sacred prostitution;

Gaia—earth worship, environmentalism, paganism, pantheism, sweat lodges;

Geb—environmental movement, animal rights, eco-paganism;

Hades—devil worship, occultism, spiritism, necromancy;

Hathor—goddess worship, earth worship, animal rights, animal worship;

Hecate—witchcraft, necromancy, crystals, spells, druidism, feminism;

Heka—mysticism, demonism, animal rights, environmentalism;

Hypnos—hypnotism, psychic dreaming, prognostication, e.s.p., clairvoyance;

Imhoteb—mystic healing, animal dancing, holistic medicine, vision quests;

Isis—wicca, witchcraft, goddess worship, magic, channeling, visualization;

Min and Qetesh—fertility rites, body worship, sensuality, pornography;

Osiris—occultianity, necromancy, anthropomorphism, occultism, spiritism;

Persephone—animism, Zoroastrianism, dualism, magic, necromancy;

Ptah—universalism, pantheism, mysticism, holistic medicine;

Sekhmet—environmentalism, mystic medicine, animal worship;

Seth—homosexuality, rebellion, earth worship, environmental movement;

Vatchit—devil worship, channeling, trancing, visualization, necromancy;

Zeus—satanism, transsexualism, pantheism, oracles, animal worship.

By whatever names they may be called, the underworld spirits, historically referred to as gods and goddesses, are gathering the combined efforts of the kingdom of Satan into a conspiracy of apocalyptic proportions. As a consequence, we are experiencing an unprecedented revival of paganism at a time when the United States is considered the most advanced economic and technological power in the world. Why paganism? There's an ominous answer. Billy Graham declares, "Lucifer, our archenemy, controls one of the most powerful and well-oiled war machines in the universe. He controls principalities, powers, and dominions. Every nation, city, village, and individual has felt the hot breath of his evil power. He is already gathering the nations of the world for the last great battle in the war against Christ—Armageddon."[13]

The following chapter will discuss paganism's ultimate contribution to the battle of Armageddon—the resurrection of the Pharaoh spirit, the human god-king.

Notes

1. Judy Vorfeld, *Joyful Woman* (July/August 1988), 15.

2. Samantha Smith, *The Eagle Forum* (Fall/Winter 1997), 20.

3. Hal Lindsey, *Planet Earth—2000 A.D.* (Palos Verdes, CA: Western Front, Ltd., 1994), 24.

4. Samantha Smith, *Goddess Earth* (Lafayette, LA: Huntington House Publishers, 1994), 80-81.

5. Carolyn R. Staffer, *Shaman's Drum* (Fall 1987), 25.

6. Richard Cavendish, *Man, Myth & Magic,* s.v. "Diana."

7. George Otis Jr., *Charisma & Christian Life* (March 1997), 54-56.

8. Randolf Price, *The Angels Within Us: A Spiritual Guide to the Twenty-Two Angels that Govern Our Lives* (New York, NY: Fawcett/Columbine/Ballantine, 1993), 2-3.

9. Raymond Moody with Paul Perry, *Reunions* (New York, NY: Villard Books, 1993), 54-62.

10. Ibid.

11. Judy Vorfeld, *Light and Life* (June 1989), 17.

12. Ibid., 17-18.

13. Billy Graham, *Angels: God's Secret Agents* (Waco, TX: Word Books, 1995), 250-251.

The New Age of the God King

"Kingship, like the gods, has for most people at most times had an appeal far profounder than its purely practical and political significance would explain: in many parts of the world kings have been reverenced as being sacred, or even divine."
—*Man, Myth & Magic*

In the near future, a man of superior intelligence, wit, charm, and diplomacy, will emerge on the world scene as a savior. He will seemingly possess a transcendent wisdom that enables him to solve problems and offer solutions to many of today's most perplexing issues. His popularity will be widespread, and his fans will include young and old, religious and non-religious, male and female. Talk show hosts will interview his colleagues, news anchors will cover his movements, scholars will applaud his uncanny ability at resolving what has escaped the rest of us, and the poor will bow down at his table. He will, in every human way, appeal to the best idea of society. But his profound comprehension and irresistible presence will be the result of an invisible network of thousands of years of collective knowledge. He will, like the pharaohs of Egypt, represent the embodiment of a very old and super-intelligent spirit. Just as Jesus Christ was the "seed of the woman" (Gen. 3:15), he will be the "seed of the serpent." Although his arrival in the form of a man was foretold by numerous Scriptures, the broad masses of the world will not recognize him as paganism's ultimate incarnation, the "beast" of Revelation 13:1.

It's been assumed for centuries that a prerequisite for the end-time Pharaoh (the Antichrist) will be a "revived" world order, an umbrella under which national boundaries dissolve, and ethnic groups, ideologies, religions, and economics from around the world, orchestrate a single and dominant sovereignty. Such a system will supposedly be free of religious and political extremes, and membership will tolerate the philosophical and cultural differences of its constituents. Except for minor nonconformities, war, intolerance, and hunger will be a thing of the past. At the head of the utopian administration, a single personality will surface. He will appear to be a man of distinguished character, but will ultimately become "a king of fierce countenance" (Dan. 8:23). With imperious decree, he will facilitate a one-world government, a universal religion, and global socialism. Those who refuse his New World Order will inevitably be imprisoned or destroyed, until at last he exalts himself "above all that is called God, or that is worshiped, so that he, as God, sitteth in the temple of God, showing himself that he is God" (2 Thess. 2:4).

For many years, the idea of an Orwellian society, where a one-world government oversees the smallest details of our lives and where human liberties are abandoned, was considered anathema. The concept that rugged individualism could be sacrificed for an anesthetized universal harmony was repudiated by America's greatest minds. Then, in the 1970s, things began to change. Following a call by Nelson Rockefeller for the creation of a "new world order,"[1] presidential candidate Jimmy Carter campaigned, saying, "We must replace balance of power politics with world order politics."[2] Evidently he struck a chord with world leaders. During the 1980s, President George Bush continued the one-world dirge by announcing over national television that "a new world order" had arrived. Following the initial broadcast, President Bush addressed Congress and made the additional comment:

> What is at stake is more than one small country [Kuwait], it is a big idea—a new world order, where diverse nations are drawn together in common cause to achieve the universal aspirations of mankind: peace and security, freedom, and the rule of law. Such is a world worthy of our struggle, and worthy of our childrens' future![3]

Ever since the President's astonishing newscast, a parade of political and religious leaders has discharged a profusion of New Age rhetoric aimed at implementing the goals of the New World Order. Al Gore, in his book *Earth In the Balance*, wrote that "we must all become partners in a bold effort to change the very foundation of our civilization." The director of the United Nations World Health Organization, Brock Chisolm, announced: "To achieve world government, it [will

be] necessary to remove from the minds of men
their individualism, loyalty to family traditions,
national patriotism."[4]

And New Age guru Benjamin Creme hit the
nail on the head by admitting: "What is the plan?
It includes the installation of a new world government and a new world religion under Maitreia."[5]
(Maitreia is a New Age "messiah.")

Concurrent with the political aspects of the
New World Order is the syncretistic and spiritual
goals of the New Age Movement. The blending of
politics and spirituality, such as occurs in New Age
mysticism, harmonizes perfectly with the ideas of
an end-time marriage of governmental policy and
religious creed as was prophesied in the Bible. To
that end, the tools necessary for paganism's ultimate incarnation, the god-king of the Great Tribulation (Satan in flesh), are in place. The "gods"
have been revived through modern mysticism. The
pagan agenda of governing by "divine representation" is being constructed. The governments of
the world are uniting beneath a one-world ban-
ner, and the earths masses stand at the brink of a
decisive moment in time.

In his book, *The New World Order,* Pat Robertson
sees the strategy of the coming world leader played
out in the following way:

> It is as if a giant plan is unfolding, every-
> thing perfectly on cue. Europe sets the date
> for its union. Communism collapses. A
> hugely popular war is fought in the Middle
> East. The United Nations is rescued from
> scorn by an easily swayed public. A new
> world order is announced. Christianity has
> been battered in the public arena, and New

The New Age of the God King169

> Age religions are in place in the schools and corporations, and among the elite. Then a financial collapse accelerates the move toward a world money system.
>
> The United States . . . turns its defense requirements over to the United Nations, along with its sovereignty. The United Nations severely limits property rights and clamps down on all Christian evangelism and Christian distinctives under the Declaration of the Elimination of All Forms of Intolerance and Discrimination Based on Religious Belief already adopted by the General Assembly. . . . Then the New Age religion of humanity becomes official, and the new world order leaders embrace it. Then they elect a world president with plenary powers who is totally given to the religion of humanity.[6]

Who will be enthroned as the President of the New World Order? Lord Maitreia? United Nations Secretary General Boutros Boutros-Ghali? A resurrected John F. Kennedy? The Pope? A complete unknown? I do not know. But an ancient scheme is unfolding. At the core of the conspiracy, a leader of indescribable brutality is scheduled to appear. He will make the combined depravities of Antiochus Epiphenes, Hitler, Stalin, and Genghis Khan, all of whom were types of the antichrist, look like child's play. He will raise his fist, "speaking great things . . . in blasphemy against God, to blaspheme his name, and his tabernacle, and them that dwell in heaven" (Rev. 13:5-6). He will champion worship of the "old gods" and "cause that as many as would not worship the image of the beast should be killed" (Rev. 13:15), and he will revive an ancient mystery religion that is "the habitation of devils, and the hold of every foul spirit, and a cage of every unclean and hateful bird" (Rev. 18:2). Such verses are reminiscent of the Mystery religions of Dionysus and Demeter, in which the Greek god Pan, a consort of Dionysus, was famous for his pandemonium ("all the devils"). The coming world religion will be similar to the Dionysian cult in that those who reject the will of the New Age god-king will be destroyed.

Pandemonium! The Pagan Gospel of the New Age God King

The gospel, according to the New Age Movement, is an expansive idea centered around the birth of a new world "consciousness." As a religion of monism (all is one), New Agers hope to accomplish what the builders of the Tower of Babel failed to do: unify the masses of the world under a single religious umbrella, and, at the macro level, harmonically converge the world's energies with the power of Gaia. To promote such goals, New Agers claim that God is pantheistic *(God is all and all is God)* and that humans are divine members of the whole "that God is." According to New Ageism, Jesus came to reveal this pantheistic nature of God and to teach humanity the gospel of Self-Realization. After illustrating the divine principle of "God within us all," Jesus ascended to a place of distinction to live among the Masters of the Spiritual Hierarchy, including Buddha and Krishna. Jesus promised that the essence of God would be revealed from time to time, and, thus, New Agers look for the imminent appearing of a

World Teacher who will, as Jesus did, illustrate the divine human potential. In this way, New Age theology prepares the world for the coming of the False Prophet and the Antichrist.

Pagans claim such a religion of Self-realization, a belief that will be championed by the Antichrist, is older than Christianity. That's true. The gospel according to the New Age Movement, a gospel of "becoming god," is as old as the fall of man. It began when the serpent said to the woman "ye shall be as gods" (Gen. 3:5), and it will culminate during the reign of the Tribulation god-king. The New Age movement provides the perfect creed for implementing such an end-time religion. It unifies the religions of the world. It consecrates the forces of nature. It provides for human divinity, and it is vogue, post modern, and politically correct. Tal Brooke, former New Age disciple of Hindu holy man, Sai Baba, confirms that "the New Age movement, and its progeny, Gaia, are spiritually correct for a new world order. Christianity is not."[7] Thus, history repeats itself, and the ancient Egyptian gospel of men becoming "gods" is fashionable again! Consequently, New Age celebrities such as Shirley MacLaine represent themselves as "I AM that I AM" at human potential symposiums around the world, and the Vice President of the United States, Al Gore, describes God in terms of "a constant and holy spiritual presence in all people, all life, and all things."[8] Hillary Clinton channels the spirits of the dead and members of the House of Representatives warn Congress of "increasing evidence of a government-sponsored religion in America . . . [a] cloudy mixture of New Age mysticism, Native American folklore and primitive earth worship."[9]

For many years, Christians wondered how the Antichrist would deceive the earth's masses. How does one convince millions of people, especially in countries where Christianity exists, to exchange their souls for temporary earthly benefits? Then, the New Age Movement came along with its focus on human-potential and self-empowerment and successfully drew many Christians away from Christ-exalting doctrines. Old-fashioned gospel preaching was replaced with positive thinking, self-realization, and pop psychology, and mystical experiences which tantalize the flesh, were sanctioned as "the last great revival." As a result, celebrity preachers advance sermons focusing on "the inner self," and Sunday morning services begin with shouts of "Are you ready for God to do great things!?" The implication that God will meet with believers and grant their many requests is touted as dynamic Christianity. The days of unconditional Christian devotion are threatened as contemporary congregations expect God to "manifest" Himself and please the whims of the audience. Although Jesus warned of an "evil and adulterous generation [that] seeketh after a sign," physical and mystical "thrills" have become the benchmark of many popular Christian gathering places. The result is a growing superficiality among some Christians who are preoccupied with mysticism and "me-ism."

As a businessman and ministry leader, I've tasted the bitter results of the "new age" segment of Christianity. Too often, these believers fall, flop, quiver, shake, and gyrate on Sunday, but can't get out of bed and go to work Monday morning. Among such employees, I've found insignificant character differences between religious groups, and "Christians" have been just as likely as non-believers to lie, cheat, and steal at my place of business. Perhaps I've been unlucky, or maybe, as I believe, twenty years of popular New Age metaphysical focusing on "self" has so impacted this generation that many "Christians" are willing to dilute their character to acquire what pleases them. Either way, an inward-focusing generation of "religious people" willing to trade their soul for whatever makes them happy is exactly what is necessary for the appearance of Antichrist. "You can stamp my hand if you'll give me what I want" is the required attitude. While many Christians and New Age devotees are sincere, giving people, the lasting result of the New Age Movement is nevertheless demonic, self-absorbed, and paves the way for the coming of paganism's preeminent materialization, the god-king of the Great Tribulation.

New Age Angels and the Chariot of the God King

When I was a child, my father made an amazing discovery while deer hunting in the mountains of Arizona. Several large and perfectly spherical craters, perhaps twenty feet across and eight feet deep, were located in an unexplored section of the range where he was hunting. The mysterious cavities were so precise that it looked as if an enormous white-hot ball had pushed into the rock, and the finish on the walls was such that rainwater filled the orbs. The sides of the holes were slick and each "pool" contained deer that had fallen in and drowned while attempting to drink the water.

Dad took pictures of the obscure semispherical holes (he showed them to the family and I remember being especially impressed), and led a representative of the Army Corps of Engineers to the location. The origin of the puzzling craters was never determined, and the Corps of Engineers filled the pools with rock to protect the wildlife. A local newspaper ran an article on the baffling holes, reprinted photographs of my father kneeling beside the orbs, and that seemed to be the end of the story.

Then, on 5 November 1975, along the north-eastern ridge of an Arizona mountain range, Travis Walton stepped out of his pick-up to look at a mysterious glowing object. While a crew of loggers waited nearby, Travis approached the UFO and was jolted by a blast of inexplicable energy. As his companions fled in terror, Travis was taken on-board the alien spacecraft and subjected to a variety of physical examinations. His story, *Fire in the Sky*, is now a motion picture. It reports what's considered to be the best documented account of a UFO abduction ever recorded. Is Travis Walton's story true? Was there a connection between the Walton-UFO and the mysterious mountain holes? Did the experiences of my sister who saw small alien-like creatures around her bed at night for years following the discovery mean anything? I don't know. But the strange phenomenon known as UFO activity is sure to play a part in the coming World Order and in the introduction of the New Age god-king.

As mentioned in chapter one, I believe a portion of UFO activity is demonic. Increasingly, others agree with that opinion. Hal Lindsey states,

"I have become thoroughly convinced that UFOs are real. . . . I believe these beings are not only extraterrestrial but supernatural in origin. To be blunt, I think they are demons."[10] In *Angels Dark and Light,* Gary Kinnaman claims, "I am fairly convinced that . . . UFO sightings are the manifestations of angels of darkness. My main reason for thinking this is that UFO sightings have never, at least to my knowledge, led a person closer to God. In fact, most UFO experiences have just the opposite effect."[11] UFO celebrity and author of *Communion* (bestselling book about his alleged alien abduction), Whitley Streiber, describes UFOnauts in terms of demonology.

He writes:

> There are worse things than death, I sus-
> pected. And I was beginning to get the
> distinct impression that one of them had
> taken an interest in me. So far the word
> demon had never been spoken among the
> scientists and doctors who were working
> with me. And why should it have been? We
> were beyond such things. We were a group
> of atheists and agnostics, far too sophisti-
> cated to be concerned with such archaic
> ideas as demons and angels."[12]

Associate professor of psychology Elizabeth L. Hillstrom points out that a growing number of academics support the conclusion that UFOnauts are synonymous with historical demons. In her informative book, *Testing the Spirits,* she writes:

> From a Christian perspective, Vallee's ex-
> planation of UFOs is the most striking
> because of its parallels with demonic activ-
> ity. UFO investigators have noticed these

similarities. Vallee himself, drawing from extrabiblical literature on demonic activities, establishes a number of parallels between UFOnauts and demons. . . . Pierre Guerin, a UFO researcher and a scientist associated with the French National Council for Scientific Research, is not so cautious: "The modern UFOnauts and the demons of past days are probably identical." Veteran researcher John Keel, who wrote *UFOs: Operation Trojan Horse* and other books on the subject, comes to the same conclusion: "The UFO manifestations seem to be, by and large, mere minor variations of the age-old demonological phenomenon."[13]

It's easy to believe that demons are involved with "flying saucers." Evil spirits can manipulate energy and matter, and the theological terms, "Transmogrification" and "Poltergeist" ("noisy ghost"), imply that spirits can make lights go off and on, doors bang, icons bleed, and saucers fly.

But if a portion of "flying saucer" activity is demonic, what nefarious purpose is served by the stealthy nature of UFO phenomena? The answer is diabolical. UFO-ism seems to be aimed at preparing the earth for the coming of Antichrist, i.e., an extraterrestrial "visitation of the gods," and, more importantly, at changing our religious beliefs. This occurs in two ways: First, from a technological standpoint, UFO sightings challenge the claim of human superiority and dispute our unique role in the universe. We are made to feel shallow, undeveloped, unenlightened. Second, from a religious point of view, extraterrestrials bring a message (as reported in hundreds of abduction cases) of easy universalism and New Age mysticism including dialogue of humans "on the verge of extraordinary telepathic and technological growth." Benevolent ETs profess to watch over us and promise to appear at the appropriate time to assist in our next big evolutionary, spiritual, and technological step forward. To prepare us for their coming, popular movies, bestselling books, cultural trends, and religious ideas, focus the earths masses on "help from above," and New Agers smile and explain "It's okay, they've been here before" and "Don't worry, ancient men simply described flying saucers in terms of demons, angels, and gods, because they didn't understand what they were seeing."

In other words, New Agers believe that space vehicles manipulating laws of physics (suddenly appearing and disappearing, operating anti-gravitationally, etc.) were assigned "god" or "angel" status by sincere but ignorant prophets, and that Ezekiel's living creatures will return someday in wheels "in the middle of a wheel" providing explanations of our origin and solutions to our problems. Such New Age claims of extraterrestrials visiting the earth in ancient times and interacting with men is biblically and historically true. Where Christians differ from New Agers is in the definition of who these creatures were and what they were doing. In the *Interlinear Hebrew Bible* we read:

> The benei Elohim saw the daughters of Adam, that they were fit extensions. And they took wives for themselves from all those that they chose ... The Nephelim were in the earth in those days, and even

afterwards when the benei Elohim came in
to the daughters of Adam, and they bore to
them—they were Powerful Ones which existed from ancient times, the men of name.
(Gen. 6:2,4)

As noted in the first two chapters of this book,
the benei Elohim were "extraterrestrial" angelic
creatures also known as "watchers," "sons of God,"
and "rephiam." They visited the earth during antiquity and used the daughters of Adam as "fit
extensions" or instruments through which they
extended themselves into the physical world. They
sought to corrupt the bloodline of Adam, to deceive the human race, and to prevent the birth of
the Messiah. They represented themselves as
"gods," and their offspring, the Nephilim ("fallen
ones"), attempted to exterminate the people of
Yahweh. In what may be a prophecy of end-time
UFOs, Isaiah connected the benei Elohim to "fiery flying seraph." We read, "Do not rejoice O
Philistia, all of you, for the rod of your striking is
broken, because a viper (Antichrist) comes forth
from the root of the snake (Satan) and his fruit is
the fiery flying seraph" (Isa. 14:29). The seraph
(seraphim) were powerful angels known for their
brilliance. If, as we suspect, some of the seraphim
followed Lucifer in the fall, it could be that such
"fiery flying seraph" are the source of UFOs today. As previously noted; the "air" above the earth
was considered by ancient Hebrew scholars to be
the dwelling place of fallen angels. An interesting
point of this is made by J. N. Schofield in *Man,
Myth & Magic:*

The warm interest of angels in mans' welfare is vividly expressed in the saying of

Jesus that there is joy before the angels of God over one sinner who repents' (Luke 15), and that children have their guardian angels standing as favoured envoys near God Himself (Matthew 18). It was through Jewish Christians that angeology, based on the Old Testament and other Jewish writings, entered the teaching of the Church. Angels were set over the life of Nature, and over human communities. God was Israel's portion but Michael was her protector, taught her Hebrew and gave the law on Sinai. Every individual had his guardian angel and babies exposed or aborted were cared for by guardian angels. There continued to be angelic intercessors and messengers of revelation or warning, but further functions were more specialized. There was an Angel of Repentance who brought to man consciousness of sin and the promise of forgiveness, and an Angel of Peace received the soul as it left the body and bore it to paradise. The Angel of Death in Sheol was a good angel and guardian of souls.

Angelic rank was associated with speculation about the universe, which increased to the three heavens known to St. Paul. All these were thought to be above the firmament [the kosmos] where fallen angels were imprisoned, and all were inhabited exclusively by angels, the lower heavens by those in charge of human affairs, the upper by Angels of the Presence. According to some speculation, these heavens (the *Hajoth-Hakados*) were successive stages through which souls must pass, encountering their guardian angels to whom account must be given.

If it's true that fallen angels inhabit the earths atmosphere and that, historically, they conducted genetic experiments on the daughters of Adam and thereby produced the mutant nephilim, does the prophecy of Jesus in Luke 17:26 indicate such activity would reoccur before the Rapture? Does recent UFO abduction activity point to genetic engineering of a new race of anti-God warriors (nephilim) as we approach the Great Tribulation? Will UFOs provide the grand entry of the ultimate cross-mutation of angelic and human species, the god-king of the New World Order? Time will tell. Until then:

> The mystery of iniquity doth already work: only he who now letteth will let, until he be taken out of the way. And then shall that wicked be revealed, whom the Lord shall consume with the spirit of his mouth, and shall destroy with the brightness of his coming: Even him, whose coming is after the working of Satan with all power and signs and lying wonders. (2 Thess. 2:7-9)

The Real War of the Worlds

In a popular New Age book on angels we read:

> Even in this day and age, films like *The Omen, Rosemary's Baby,* and *The Seventh Sign* evoke horror, because they tap into the possibility that we may be influenced in some way by universal messengers of evil. However, according to our angelic informants [?], the situation, thank God, is not

> like that at all. . . . Slowly, surely, we are collectively emerging from this *illusion of evil*. . . . Many contemporary Christians have begun to abandon the concept that there is a real devil, recognizing once again that there is only one omnipotent force in the universe [emphasis added].[14]

Whereas some pagans profess a belief in Karma or Zoroastrianism (opposing forces of good and evil), the idea of personal evil spirits such as Satan and his angels is rejected by New Agers. The concepts of Hell and a future Great Judgment are also disregarded. But the reality of Hell and the doom of Satan's followers is nevertheless described in the Bible. The "old gods" of the underworld, including Zeus, Apollo, Demeter, Isis, and others, will be judged by Yahweh. "The Lord will be terrible unto them: for he will famish all the gods of the earth" (Zeph. 2:11). "The Lord of hosts, the God of Israel, saith; Behold, I will punish the . . . gods" (Jer. 46:25). Yahweh will also punish the leader of the gods, that old serpent, called the Devil, and his human followers. In Isaiah we read:

> Come, my people, enter thou into thy chambers, and shut thy doors about thee: hide thyself as it were for a little moment, until the indignation be overpast. For, behold, the Lord cometh out of his place to punish the inhabitants of the earth for their iniquity: the earth also shall disclose her blood, and shall no more cover her slain. In that day the Lord with his sore and great and strong sword shall punish Leviathan the piercing serpent, even Leviathan that crooked serpent; and he shall slay the dragon that is in the sea. (Isa. 26:20-27:1)

However futile, the gods will retaliate, and a war of indescribable intensity will occur in the future. It will be fought on land and sea, in the heavens above, and in the earth below, in the physical and spiritual worlds. It will include "Michael and his angels [fighting] against the dragon; and the dragon [fighting] and his angels" (Rev. 12:7). Heretics will join the battle and call upon "idols of gold, and silver, and brass, and stone, and of wood" (Rev. 9:20) to convene their evil powers against the Christian God, and New Agers will unite with "unclean spirits like frogs. . . . the spirits of devils [the frog goddesses Heka or Hekate?] working miracles, which go forth unto the kings of the earth . . . to gather them to the battle of that great day. . . . [to] a place called in the Hebrew tongue Armageddon ["Mount Megiddo"]" (Rev. 16:13-14;16). There, in the valley of Megiddo, the omnipotent Christ will utterly repel the forces of darkness and destroy the New World army. Blood will flow like rivers, and the fowl of the air will "eat the flesh of the mighty, and drink the blood of the princes of the earth."

Tim LaHaye says, "As far back as the time of Napoleon, that great valley was claimed to be the most natural battleground of the whole earth."[15] Besides Armageddon, battles will be fought in the Valley of Jehoshaphat and in the city of Jerusalem. But the battle of Armageddon will climax the hostility between God Almighty and the lower gods of the underworld. Once before, Satan and his "god" spirits challenged Yahweh at Megiddo. They lost. On Mount Carmel, overlooking the Valley of Armegeddon, the prophets of the demon-god Baal dared the Hebrew God to answer by fire. He did and He will again. When He does, where will you be? Will you join forces with the gods of the underworld and trust in the armies of the New Age/ New World Order? If so, here is your future:

> And I saw the beast, and the kings of the earth, and their armies, gathered together to make war against him that sat on the horse [Jesus], and against his army [Christians and angels of God]. And the beast was taken, and with him the false prophet that wrought miracles before him, with which he deceived them that had received the mark of the beast, and them that worshipped his image. These both were cast alive into a lake of fire burning with brimstone. And the remnant were slain with the sword of him that sat upon the horse, which sword proceeded out of his mouth: and all the fowls were filled with their flesh. . . . And I saw a great white throne, and him that sat on it, from whose face the earth and the heaven fled away: and there was found no place [to hide]. And I saw the dead, small and great, stand before God; and the books were opened: and another book was opened, which is the book of life: and the dead were judged out of those things which were written in the books, according to their works. . . . And whosoever was not found written in the book of life was cast into the lake of fire. (Rev.19:19-21; 20:11-12,15)

If you repent of your sins and believe on the Lord Jesus Christ you will experience a different destiny at the battle of Armageddon:

And I saw heaven opened, and behold a
white horse; and he that sat upon him was
called Faithful and True [Jesus], and in
righteousness he doth judge and make war.
His eyes were as a flame of fire, and on his
head were many crowns; and he had a name
written, that no man knew, but he himself.
And he was clothed with a vesture dipped
in blood: and his name is called The Word
of God. And the armies which were in
heaven [Christians and angels of God] followed him upon white horses, clothed in
fine linen, white and clean. And out of his
mouth goeth a sharp sword, that with it he
should smite the nations: and he shall rule
them with a rod of iron: and he treadeth
the winepress of the fierceness and wrath
of Almighty God. And he hath on his thigh
a name written, KING OF KINGS, AND
LORD OF LORDS. . . . And I saw a new
heaven and a new earth: for the first heaven
and the first earth were passed away;
and. . . . I heard a great voice out of heaven
saying, Behold, the tabernacle of God is
with men. . . . And God shall wipe away all
tears from their eyes; and there shall be no
more death, neither sorrow, nor crying,
neither shall there be any more pain: for
the former things are passed away. And he
that sat upon the throne said. . . . I will give
unto him that is a thirst of the fountain of
the water of life freely. He that overcometh
shall inherit all things; and I will be his
God, and he shall be my son [or daughter]
(Rev. 19:11-16; 20:1-7).

Preceding such apocalypse, the year 2000 will undoubtedly herald the unprecedented changes of a final millennium. As the gods of the underworld work to establish dominion over mankind and within a new world order, the god-king (Antichrist) of the Great Tribulation will prepare for his appearance. Such is a time for Christians worldwide to unite in common cause. What can believers do about the spread of paganism and the goals of a New World Order?

First, Christians must resist the temptation to squander their time and energy pursuing silly mystical experiences and religious entertainment and wholly commit to the vocal community declaration of the Gospel of Jesus Christ. It is the preaching of the Gospel that embodies the power of God unto salvation; both of nations and of individuals.

Second, we must be willing to intercede in prayer and fasting for our nation and for its leaders. The lower gods of the underworld and their impact on society have historically been overcome by heavenly activity generated by righteous men and women on bended knees.

Third, political representatives need to hear about Christian concerns. A single call or letter is considered by most congressmen to represent the will of many thousands of other Americans.

Fourth, let's prepare for the coming of Christ! Believers in this age need to draw close to God and to His Word and live righteously. As R.L. Brandt said in the foreword, "We are at the end of the age. The coming of our Lord is near. Let us sound the trumpet in Zion!"

A Word from Ex New-Ager Judy Vorfeld

"Everything is about power," says a character in a best-selling novel. This certainly appears to be the key theme of the Bible. God the Father, God the Son, and God the Holy Spirit, from the beginning, have all power, and, in their holiness, are worthy of the highest form of worship.

Early in the Bible we see Satan working relentlessly to become the only object of worship on Planet Earth. Fully aware of the nature and purposes of Jesus, Satan still tried to manipulate Him into worshipping him. Matthew 4:8 reveals that Satan "took Him to a very high mountain, and showed Him all the kingdoms of the world, and their glory; and he said to Him, 'All these things will I give You, if You fall down and worship me.' "

Through the centuries, the enemy downplays God's power and the work of the Cross. He continues to work vigorously to make Jesus an equal of Buddha, Mohammed, the Dalai Lama, and other wise ones. He often succeeds. But Christians know that Jesus came to Earth to die, not to teach platitudes or become politically correct. God didn't plan that Jesus would be on the *All-time List of the World's Greatest Teachers* or become *Time* magazine's Person of the Year.

Many people we love have fallen under the influence of deceived teachers and deceptive philosophies. Their doctrines, often graced with biblical words and phrases, undermine God's authority, ability, promises and power. These people cling to religion, hoping for peace, happiness, and meaning for their lives. They honestly believe that religious practices will accomplish this. At one time, so did I, ignorant of the fact that Satan offers a highway to happiness paved with empty promises and cheap glitter. Some of the road signs say, *This Way To A God Who Won't Embarrass You* (subtitle: Forget This "Born Again" Nonsense), *Turn Left For The God Of Your Design,* and *Two Miles To An Intellectually Stimulating God.* Countless souls struggle on this wide, but crowded, road.

God offers a slim, straight highway of simple faith, paved with the blood of Jesus, and ending at Calvary. Christianity offers a spiritual life based on what Christ did 2,000 years ago. Beyond the requirement of belief, God offers something quite different than all other religions: relationship.

I grew up thinking that Christianity required good works and constant church attendance. I also thought God was watching me with a lightning bolt in one hand and a sledge hammer in the other, waiting to get me if I misbehaved. After moving from Humanism to the New Age Movement to Christianity, I discovered that going to church was a choice and a privilege, but my eternal destiny wasn't based on how many times a week I attended church. Relationship with God, not religion, is everything.

Part of a healthy relationship comes from listening well, and I'm not always the best listener. God's voice is soft and gentle. I've learned that He loves me deeply and passionately. He shows it many times each day in tiny, precious ways. His delight in me helps me see myself through His eyes as one who is lovable. I've always been able to see the value and beauty in others, but not in myself.

How has He revealed Himself to me? Perhaps

the best example is in filling a basic need, of having a loving relationship with my father. For most of my life, my father and I were strangers, and I had a hole in my soul. My parents divorced when I was a teen. I've been close to my mother most of my life; she's a friend and a delight. But by the time Dad reached 90, I figured things would always be the same. I loved him, but didn't know him. Several years ago, his family, converging from many parts of the country, and including many great grandchildren, threw a surprise 90th birthday party for him. I believe this activated something deep inside him. The following year, I flew up from Arizona to visit him in Washington. For a solid week, we lugged cameras, maps, and sack lunches, hiking to many breathtaking locations. Actually, I hiked. Sometimes Dad (who has Congestive Heart Failure) crawled. We laughed a lot.

This visit triggered something in both of us, and our relationship began to change. Most of our contact since then has been via telephone. How can I express my feelings when my 94-year-old father says, "I love you, darling," as our conversations come to a close? His voice seems coated with honey. My heart bubbles with joy. I always hang up the phone in awe of a Heavenly Father that allowed this to happen. Would I have loved God as much if Dad had died before our special reconciliation? Absolutely. But God gave me a special gift, a just-for-Judy gift, another taste of his grace.

Christians, are any of your loved ones traveling the highway of futility? Are they trapped in paganism? Do you feel frustrated in your inability to share Jesus with them? Here are a few things you can do that may help them see the truth:

Intercede. Ask God to help you see them from His perspective, to feel what He feels toward them. Be willing to have your heart broken with love as you experience God's deep, powerful love for them.

Never stop praying for them. My family and Christian friends lifted me up before the Lord (some, for years) before I accepted Him.

Separate the believer from the belief, but be willing to be totally honest in discussing those beliefs, if God makes an opening.

Resist shooting them with "Bible Bullets," but know your Bible well, and be prepared to share the truth when the opening comes. If you are not a Christian, I ask one thing: on your own, begin reading the Bible, with the understanding that it may be more than an ordinary book and more than mere words. Consider reading, each day, about six chapters in the Old Testament to two in the New Testament, starting with Genesis and Matthew. Read it with this in mind: *does it reveal Jesus Christ as God's Son, and does it show how He made a way for you to have a deeply intimate relationship with Him?* Surely you can take time to read this book and see if it has truth and consistency running through it.

There is much truth in the statement that everything is about power. We humans constantly look for it in our lives. Anything we can understand, we can control (to one extent or another). This is why it is important for so many to have a god they can figure out. Many sincere people search in vain for a magic blueprint for happiness and meaning to life. One road offers any kind of a god you want. Pick from the gods of the past, the gods of the New Age, or go the create-a-god route: choose size, shape, age, race, gender, and composition.

The other road is just wide enough for one person at a time. At the end is Jesus. His open arms reach toward the traveler. All He offers is two nail-scarred hands.

Notes

1. Pat Robertson, *The New World Order* (Dallas, TX: Word Publishing, 1991), 5.

2. Ibid., 6.

3. Ibid., 14.

4. Ibid., 7.

5. Ibid., 6.

6. Ibid., 176-177.

7. Ibid., 167-168.

8. Al Gore, *Earth In the Balance* (Boston, MA: Houghton Mifflin Company, 1992), 368.

9. Jayne Schindler, *The Eagle Forum* (Fall/Winter 1997), 16.

10. Lindsey, *Planet Earth 2000 A.D.*, 68.

11. Gary Kinnaman, *Angels Dark and Light* (Ann Arbor, MI: Servant Publications, 1994), 132-133.

12. Whitley Streiber, *Communion* (William Morrow, NY: Beech Tree Books, 1987).

13. Elizabeth L. Hillstrom, *Testing the Spirits* (Downers Grove, IL: InterVarsity Press, 1995) 207-208.

14. Alma Daniel, Timothy Wyllie, and Andrew

Ramer, *Ask Your Angels: A Practical Guide to Working with the Messengers of Heaven to Empower and Enrich Your Life* (New York: Ballantine Books, 1992), 39-40.

15. Tim LaHaye, *Revelation Illustrated and Made Plain* (Zondervan Publishing House, Grand Rapids, MI, 1975), 267.